Speaking 4

CAMBRIDGE SKILLS FOR FLUENCY

Cambridge Skills for Fluency is a series of supplementary materials covering the skills of listening, speaking, reading and writing; each skill is developed at four levels, from pre-intermediate through to advanced.

The series aims to develop students' confidence and fluency in English, by offering a variety of topics and activities which engage students' interest and encourage them to share their personal reactions and opinions.

Although all the books in the series share the same underlying principles, we have tried to avoid complete uniformity across the series, and so each book has its own features and its own particular approach to skills development:
- The *Listening* books aim to develop students' ability to understand real-life spoken English, through recordings of natural, spontaneous speech, selected and edited to make them accessible at each level.
- The *Speaking* books aim to develop oral fluency by focusing on topics that are personally relevant to students and which encourage students to draw on their own life experience, feelings and cultural knowledge.
- The *Reading* books aim to develop students' skill in reading English by introducing them to a wide variety of authentic texts, supported by tasks and activities designed to increase involvement and confidence in the reading process.
- The *Writing* books place writing in a central position in the language class, presenting it as a creative activity which contributes to language learning in general.

Level 4 of the series consists of the following titles:
Listening 4 by Adrian Doff and Christopher Jones
Speaking 4 by Joanne Collie and Stephen Slater
Reading 4 by Simon Greenall and Diana Pye
Writing 4 by Andrew Littlejohn

CAMBRIDGE SKILLS FOR FLUENCY
Series Editor: Adrian Doff

Speaking 4

Joanne Collie
Stephen Slater

Published by the Press Syndicate of the University of Cambridge
The Pitt Building, Trumpington Street, Cambridge CB2 1RP
40 West 20th Street, New York, NY 10011–4211, USA
10 Stamford Road, Oakleigh, Melbourne 3166, Australia

© Cambridge University Press 1993

First published 1993

Printed in Great Britain
by Scotprint Ltd, Musselburgh, Scotland

ISBN 0 521 39972 6 book
ISBN 0 521 39973 4 cassette

GO

Contents

Map of the book

Unit	Themes/Vocabulary areas	Areas of communication	Learner activities
1	Secrets, gossiping, telling 'white lies'.	Discussing opinions; reacting to case stories; expressing judgments; relating true or imaginary anecdotes.	Discussing; listening and comparing views; panel game.
2	Oral presentations, public speaking.	Building a profile of a good speaker; preparing, practising and assessing a talk; overcoming nervousness.	Completing a diagram; choosing and discussing options; giving unprepared talks in groups.
3	Stress in life and language learning; ways of reducing stress.	Gist reading and discussion; comparing experiences; choosing, trying and assessing stress-reducing methods.	Discussing an article in pairs, then groups; listening and note-taking; group experiment and assessment.
4	Politeness and rudeness.	Discussing cultural views; relating experiences; seeking and sharing information and opinions.	Small group discussion; listening and completing notes; organising a survey in class and in the community.
5	Routines at home and at work, keeping records, oral diaries.	Comparing views on personal habits, occupations; exchanging information, re-telling stories and reacting to them.	Completing a weekly planner; reading and matching; listening in pairs and re-telling; creating and sharing oral diaries.
6	Alternative lifestyles.	Discussing personal preferences; negotiating group choices in a hypothetical situation and comparing with a real life case.	Group discussion with visuals and a questionnaire; writing advice; mini-simulation based on group choices; listening, note-taking, discussing.
7	Memory and memorisation, ways of learning vocabulary.	Talking about memory; exchanging strategies on ways of remembering and experimenting with different methods; re-creating and sharing a precious memory.	Discussion based on sentence completion; a class memory test; pair discussion, whole class trial of memorising methods; pair work based on personal memories; reading a poem. Optional: creating a poem or a poster.
8	Ambition, jobs, career counselling.	Stating, justifying opinions; creating visual equivalents for experience and opinion; talking about the future and the past; preparing to give advice.	Pairwork: making, discussing lists; groupwork: making diagrams; jigsaw listening and discussion; creating a group questionnaire. Optional project extension.
9	Magic and legends from different countries.	Responding to visuals; describing cultural customs; imagining the future; sharing national legends; completing a narrative.	Guessing; sentence completion and discussion; preparation in pairs of an oral presentation; reading a story and writing an ending for it.
10	Dangers for individuals, countries and the planet.	Exchanging views on environmental problems and possible solutions; negotiating a group activity or observing and opposing; assessing different solutions.	Vocabulary, diagram work in pairs; listening with gap-filling; choosing options; forming groups based on preferences and making choices; class feedback.

Unit	Themes/Vocabulary areas	Areas of communication	Learner activities
11	Public charity and charity appeals.	Talking about personal priorities and public charities; making and justifying decisions; practising the language and techniques of persuasion.	Pair and pyramid discussion, making lists; jigsaw listening and reporting; creating a commercial in groups and performing it. Optional mini-debate.
12	Good and bad features of public buildings.	Discussing public buildings in general and in particular cases; supporting views and opinions. Optional practice of persuasion.	Pair discussion; listening and completing diagrams; pair vocabulary work, listing; class feedback; pair listening and note-taking. Optional role play game.
13	Homes of the past and the future.	Describing a room; expressing and comparing preferences; making and explaining choices; visualising, discussing the future.	Pairwork: describing a visual; discussion; listening and reacting; choosing options; group creation of an advertisement or poster.
14	Creating information guides and cassettes.	Talking about the place where you are living, finding out information about it; making the information available to others.	Small group discussion, information gathering and reporting to class; group project: preparing, writing, recording; class feedback.
15	Special needs in society.	Exchanging views about social conditions; giving reasons and justifying; negotiating group decisions.	Pair discussion based on questions, choices; listening for details, checking; groupwork on a case study.
16	Pain and disease.	Describing physical sensations; comparing experiences with and views about doctors; seeking and exchanging information or opinions; reading for interpretation and discussion.	Vocabulary work based on visuals; listening for meaning and specific words; group role play of a radio programme, class mingling; pair reading, guessing, discussion.
17	Alternative medicine.	Eliciting information and sharing ideas; reading for information; assessing different options; gathering and sharing information.	Class discussion; pairwork reading, re-telling, evaluating; jigsaw listening and note-taking; group preparation for an individual oral presentation.
18	Growing up and bringing up children.	Talking about past experiences; finding out, comparing views on upbringing; discussing traditional sayings and writing new ones. Optional: assessing, giving advice.	Completing, discussing sentences; class discussion; grading factors individually, class feedback; pairwork: matching, writing. Optional: reading a poem, advising.
19	Caring for children in difficult situations.	Considering a case study situation; reacting to developments; making and justifying decisions.	Guided simulation based on on-going listening prompts; group and class discussion.
20	Communicating and failing to communicate.	Finding out facts and reacting to them; giving reasons; working with different language registers; relating personal anecdotes; discussing cultural differences.	Class questionnaire; pair lists leading to class discussion; listening for specific information; pairwork: changing the register of messages; individual narration, class reaction and discussion.

Thanks

The authors would like to thank the following for their valuable contributions to *Speaking 4*:

Lindsay White first and foremost for her unfailing patience, help and support. Also Jeanne McCarten, Adrian Doff, Barbara Thomas, Liz Driscoll, Amanda Ogden, Peter Ducker, Peter Taylor and Sarah Almy.

Sean Power, Sunita Sehmi and their students at ELCRA Bell, Geneva, for their project and photographs included on pp. 58–9.

The authors and publishers would like to thank the following teachers and institutions for piloting *Speaking 4*:

Fiona Currie, EF International School of English, Cambridge; Norma Innes, Lilliput English Centre, Bournemouth; Peter Marron, The British Council, Madrid; David Moreton, Bell College, Saffron Walden; Sean Power, ASC Language Training, Geneva; Tony Robinson, Eurocentre, Cambridge; Carol Hunter and Heather Weyh.

1 | Secrets

Gossiping and keeping secrets

1 Delighting in idle talk

gossip /gɒsɪp/, **gossips, gossiping, gossiped**. 1 **Gossip** is informal conversation or information about other people or their actions, often including unkind or disapproving comments about their private affairs. ᴇɢ *...a nice, chatty letter full of news and gossip... ...spreading scandal and gossip about their colleagues... Gossip had it that she would marry Granby.*
2 A **gossip** is **2.1** a person who enjoys talking informally to people, especially about the private affairs of other people; used showing disapproval. ᴇɢ *Gossips have insisted that he's more than just another friend.. Isn't he a bit of a gossip himself?* **2.2** an informal conversation, especially about other people or local events. ᴇɢ *What he really enjoys is a good gossip... ...friendly gossips over our garden gates.*
3 If you **gossip**, you talk informally with someone, especially about other people or local events. ᴇɢ *Well, let us not gossip about the past... I mustn't stay gossiping with you any longer... Some gossiping old woman had seen them meet.*

Have you ever known any 'gossips'? What were they like? What did they talk about? What is your idea of a typical gossip? Build up a picture with another student. Then compare with other students in the class.

Are you a gossip? Find out how many people in your class think that:

– they are gossips (and why or why not)
– men are greater gossips than women (and why or why not)

1

2 Is gossip harmless?

Do any of the following statements sum up your opinion about gossiping?
Add your own statements if you prefer. Explain the reasons for your views.

Gossip is a good thing	*Gossip is a bad thing*
Gossips are friendly.	Gossiping is cruel and can be harmful.
Curiosity is only human.	Interfering in other people's lives is wrong.
It's a good way of getting to know people.	Gossip is the cause of friction and quarrels.
....	....

Listen to two people talking about gossiping. Do they think gossip is a
good or a bad thing overall? Do you agree with their opinions? Compare
your views.

With a partner, decide whether gossip is likely to be harmful in the following
situations.

1 Two friends at work gossip about the fact that a colleague has applied
secretly for another job.
2 A newspaper reports gossip about a government minister's affair with an
actress.
3 Someone on a radio programme hints at gossip about a leading
industrialist whose financial affairs may involve fraudulent dealings.

Try to think of at least one other similar situation to add to the list, then
compare notes with another pair of students.

3 Should you tell . . . ?

Are there times when you think it's best to tell a secret rather than keep it?
With a partner, consider these situations:

1 You go to the cinema and see your best friend's husband hugging another woman. Should you tell your friend?	2 You are shopping in a large store when you see two adolescents putting cassette tapes into their pockets. You recognise one of them as a friend's child. Should you tell your friend what you saw?	3 A friend confides that his mother's doctor has told him she has an incurable disease. The disease may progress quickly, or very slowly, but patients who are depressed often degenerate more swiftly. The mother has not yet been told and she is still reasonably fit and cheerful. Your friend asks your advice – should he tell her now and risk making her more depressed?

With your partner, choose one of the cases where you think you would tell the person concerned. Use another situation of your own if you prefer. Prepare what you would say. Decide on the strategy to adopt. Is it best to be blunt, or are you going to try and soften the truth in some way?

When you are ready, change partners. (Try to work with someone who has chosen a different case or situation.) In turn, tell each other about the situation you chose and your strategies in telling the person involved.

Optional further listening: If you like, you can listen to three people discussing similar issues. Are their opinions close to your own or quite different?

4 Are you a good liar?

To keep a secret, you sometimes have to tell 'white lies'. This seems to be easier for some people (even normally truthful people) than for others. How easy is it for you? Can you keep a straight face as you say something that is not really true? How many people in the class think they are good 'liars'?

To check whether you are a good liar or not, play this game which is sometimes played on the radio in England.

Work in groups of four or six (teams of two or three people). In your team, decide which person is going to tell a true anecdote. The other(s) will tell false ones. Plan your anecdotes together.

When everyone is ready, each team takes it in turns to tell their anecdotes. The opposing team can ask any questions they like, and the team members must answer. At the end of the set time, the opposing team guesses which person has told the true story.

2 | And now, ladies and gentlemen . . .

Making oral presentations and participating in discussions

People often have to make oral presentations – not only in language classes, but in their work or their lives. It can be daunting, even in your own language! We hope this unit will make public speaking a bit easier for you, and more enjoyable.

1 A good speaker?

What makes a speaker interesting and worth listening to? With a partner, complete this diagram showing the qualities of a good speaker.

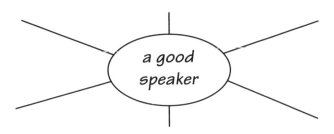

a good speaker

Compare your diagram with another pair of students. Choose the three most important qualities.

If you can, arrange to watch a talk together, e.g. a talk, a chat show, or a panel discussion on TV or video. Assess the speaker(s) according to your three criteria.

2 Preparing a talk

Good preparation is often the secret of success in giving a talk. Here are some steps which can be used in preparing yourself to give a talk. With a partner, decide which steps would be useful for someone who is going to give:

— a formal presentation within a company, at a conference, or a seminar presentation on an academic course
— an informal talk, e.g. telling a small group of students about the college facilities

(Some steps will be useful for both kinds of talks.)

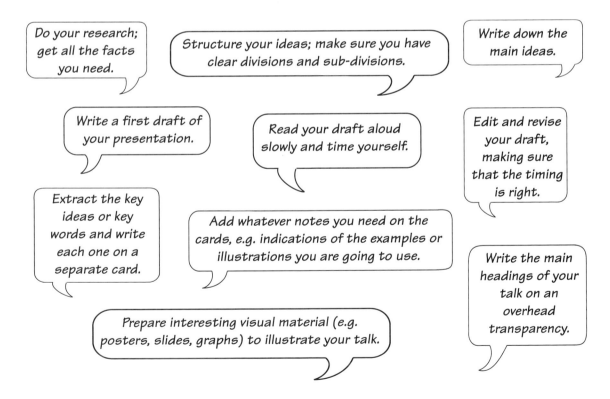

Compare your ideas with other students.

3 How to be a good speaker

Read these rules on how to become a truly rotten speaker.

How to be a truly rotten speaker

Anyone can learn to be a truly rotten speaker. Just follow these easy rules.
1 Stand or sit with your head down. Remember to keep looking at the floor.
2 If you use a microphone, turn it up to produce a high-pitched whine. Blow into it vigorously from time to time. That should keep the audience awake.
3 Read from a written text very rapidly. Mumble. Remember that a good presentation must be a bit challenging for the audience.
4 If you use an overhead projector, make sure you stand in front of it. Don't be boring – project the image on to the wall or ceiling rather than the screen.

~ ~~ ~~ful ~~ ~~~~~~ ~~ ~~ice. An even m~~~ ~~ton~

In small groups, discuss the advice you would give on 'How to be a good speaker'. Think of as many pieces of advice as you can. In your group's opinion, what is the most important rule?

4 Shall we have some practice?

Think of a controversial topic, and write one or two questions about the topic on a card or piece of paper.

Here are three examples:

1 Is it absolutely necessary for children aged 6–12 to have art and music lessons as part of their studies? Aren't these lessons just a waste of educational time?
2 Should car users be taxed very heavily because of the damage they do to the environment?
3 Do we not spend too much of our national income looking after animals? Shouldn't we ban pets and use the money on people?

In groups of about four or six, put your topic cards face down on the table in the middle. In turn, take a card from the top of the pile, read the questions, and speak on the topic for about one minute. Be sure to make eye contact at least once with every member of the group as you speak.
Others in the group: Listen and add a comment of your own, either adding another aspect to the speaker's views, or disagreeing politely.

5 Feedback (optional extension)

In groups or as a class, discuss the mini-presentation exercises you have just been doing and talk about your reactions. Can you give each other some tips on becoming better speakers? (Try to emphasise the positive. It will probably be more useful for speakers to build on their strengths first, then try to do something to reduce or compensate for their weak points.)

Share any experience you have had in overcoming nervousness. Do any of the following work for you?

1 Relaxation exercises, e.g. flexing your muscles and relaxing them, making a tight fist and then relaxing it, rotating your head slowly and shrugging your shoulders several times
2 Deep breathing, e.g. taking several deep breaths before beginning to speak
3 Role play, e.g. pretending to yourself that you are a famous, experienced speaker whom everyone is waiting impatiently to hear
4 Focusing upon the audience, e.g. trying to see them as individuals, speaking as much as possible to each one of them
5 Ignoring the audience, e.g. imagining that what you see in front of you is a lot of coconuts rather than people

3 | Stress

Stress in modern life and in the language classroom

1 Stress: is your life a blur?

You are going to read a newspaper article, in two parts, about stress.

The first part of the article deals generally with stress. Read it as quickly as you can. Help each other with any difficulties.

STRESS: IS YOUR LIFE A BLUR?

IN AMERICA they call it hurry sickness. Britain caught a bad dose of it in the 1990s. As diseases go, it's lethal: in the West, it may be the biggest killer of modern times. But it pursues its victims by stealth. You are probably suffering from it now, as you read this. What's that itch at the back of your mind, telling you all the things you should be doing? Shouldn't you be getting out, getting on, getting ahead?

The itch has a name – stress – and the world is suffering an epidemic of it. Work stress is increasing everywhere, says the International Labour Organization, because of competition and change. Surveys have found that a third of American workers seriously considered leaving their jobs last year because of it, and that one in four chief exccutives of European companies are so worried about stress that they have thought of a different career.

But you don't leave stress behind at the office. It lurks in traffic jams, crowded tubes, cancelled trains. It roars at you from motor bikes and heavy lorries, chatters at you through the letter box and over the phone, whines at you from children, barks at you from an irritable spouse. It is implicated, increasingly, in the two great 'diseases of civilisation' – cancer and heart disease – which have risen inexorably for most of this century. Stress – defined as environmental overload on an organism – works by damaging or weakening the circulatory and immune systems. Dr Audrey Livingstone Booth, of the Stress Foundation, believes that more than half of all illness reported to GPs is stress related. Cary Cooper, Professor of Organisational Psychology at the University of Manchester Institute of Science and Technology, estimates that work stress alone could cost Britain up to 10 per cent of gross national product. Yet for a disease that is so costly in economic and human terms, we have taken a long time to wake up to its dangers.

With a partner, discuss these comments on the first part of the article. Do you agree with any of them? Compare your ideas with other students.

1 The extract discusses stress as though it were a disease. This is not right. It would be more helpful to consider stress as a social condition, rather than a medical condition.

2 The extract implies that ambition is not a healthy thing. But what is wrong with it? If people don't want to be successful, they might as well be vegetables.

3 By using words like 'roars', 'chatters', 'whines' and 'barks', the extract links stress with the noise of modern life. In fact the younger generation, the generation of loud rock music, loves noise, so how can noise cause stress?

4 The extract makes a link between stress and two dangerous diseases, cancer and heart disease. The link is not proven. In fact the diseases are more likely to be linked to diet.

5 This extract may be appropriate for Britain or the USA, but it does not apply to our country.

The second part of the article gives some tips to help people cope with stress in modern life. Read it as quickly as you can.

How to avoid hurry sickness and lead a better life

★ Simplify your life. Avoid machines of all kinds. Buy fewer things.
★ Throw away unnecessary documents.
★ Get regular fresh air.
★ Don't use a car. Take public transport.
★ Go for country walks. Nature is the most neglected therapy of all.
★ Avoid long-distance commuting. Work and shop near your home.
★ Go home from work earlier. Long hours don't make you more efficient.
★ Get more sleep. Lack of it lowers your resistance to disease.
★ Stop watching your watch. Don't cram your schedules. Stop pacing, seething or twitching.
★ Take all your holidays.
★ Relax, play sport or music, develop a hobby.
★ Exercise regularly. Eat sensibly. Don't smoke, drink alcohol moderately.
★ Laugh. Don't bottle things up. Talk to someone.
★ Co-operate, don't compete.
★ Plant a tree and watch it grow.

⫸→

Have you or anyone you know ever suffered from 'hurry sickness'? Can you think of a time in the future when it might be a problem for you?

With another student, talk about each tip and choose the three which you think are most appropriate and helpful. Have you ever used any of these tips yourself? Did they work?

When you are ready, work with another pair of students and compare your ideas and your choice of tips.

2 Yoga helps me to relax

The bow

The bow (or dhanurasana) should be performed as an extension of the cobra and involves raising both the upper and lower body simultaneously to stretch and strengthen the back muscles and flex the spine. The bow also tones the liver and bowels, and reduces tension and menstrual cramp. Once you have mastered the bow, you can increase these benefits by rocking gently back and forward on your abdomen. Beginners will find it easier to do this with legs lifted slightly apart.

1 *Lie flat with your head down. Inhale and bend your knees up, then grasp your ankles and exhale.*

2 *Inhaling, lift your head and chest while pulling on your ankles, to raise your trunk and thighs off the floor. Hold for 3 breaths then relax.*

Listen to some people comparing the ways they cope with stress and make notes on the ways they mention.

In your group, compare the notes you made about the speakers. Do you agree with them about the best ways of coping with stress?

3 Stress in language learning

In recent years, psychologists and linguists have become interested in the stress involved in language learning. Talk about these questions with other students:

— You have now been learning English for some time. Have you found it stressful?
— What do you think are the main causes of stress in language learning? Compare your experiences and try to list as many causes of stress as you can.
— What remedies can you think of for this particular form of stress? Are any of the general tips you discussed of any use? What particular advice would you have for language learners?

4 Remedies for stress in language learning

Here are a few methods that have sometimes been proposed to help reduce the stress caused by language learning. Read and discuss them with another student.

1 **Listening to music.** Put on a cassette of very soft soothing music. On another cassette player, put on a tape with a long passage of the foreign language on it. Try to adopt as comfortable a position as you possibly can – lie down if at all possible. Close your eyes and listen. Don't worry if you don't understand everything. Don't even worry if you fall asleep. Repeat this for at least ten minutes at the beginning of every class.

2 **Relaxing exercises.** Stretch, rotate head and shoulders. Flex your arm muscles, then relax. Make a tight fist, then relax. Stretch your legs out, then relax. Take a deep breath, hold it for five seconds, then exhale slowly. Do these exercises before each class.

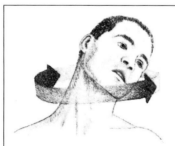

Head rolls
Roll your head slowly clockwise and then counter-clockwise, three times each way, allowing it to drop heavily.

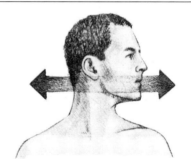

Turning the head
Keeping your head level, turn it side to side ten times slowly, then ten times more quickly.

⫸➤

3 **Non-verbal warming-up exercises.** Use these to reduce tension at the beginning of a class.

e.g. *Handshakes*

Everyone walks freely about the room. The object is to shake hands with everyone in the room, without speaking, but with an appropriate facial expression. (Instructions may be given which involve a change in expression, e.g. 'Each person you shake hands with is a very good friend', 'You are at a very formal reception where you do not know any of the people you meet'.)

or *Hand catching*

In pairs, students stand facing each other. One person holds out both hands, about 25 cm apart. The other person tries to pass a hand vertically between his or her partner's hands without getting caught in the trap, which can of course close at any time. When a hand is caught, the partners reverse roles.

(from Maley and Duff, *Drama Techniques in Language Learning*)

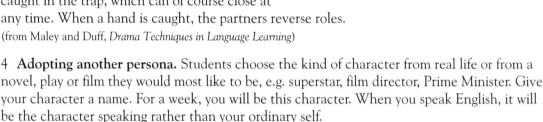

4 **Adopting another persona.** Students choose the kind of character from real life or from a novel, play or film they would most like to be, e.g. superstar, film director, Prime Minister. Give your character a name. For a week, you will be this character. When you speak English, it will be the character speaking rather than your ordinary self.

5 **An organised 'whinge'.** Set aside at least fifteen minutes every week at the end of the language period. Work in groups of three or four. During those fifteen minutes, encourage everyone to speak their mind very openly about that week's language classes. Were the classes interesting or boring? Were they frustrating? What did everyone least enjoy? What did they find most difficult? The teacher can listen if the group allows it, but never speaks. This has to be done regularly over a period of at least four weeks. The group can decide whether to use English or their own language if they all have the same mother tongue.

6 **No-correction time.** Have part of a lesson each week during which it is agreed by the class that there will be no correction of language used. This period is for fluency practice, using the units of this book, for example.

Try one of the methods in your class.

Then meet in groups of three or four to talk about the results. Do you feel that the method was successful?

One spokesperson from each group: Report to the whole class. Try to establish a class profile of your feelings about the experiment.
Do you want to continue it? Or would you like to try another of the methods?

4 | Well brought up?

Politeness and rudeness

1 It's the height of rudeness!

In your country, which of the following things are considered rude? Add two other items from your own country to the list. Label each item a) very rude, b) a bit rude, c) not rude at all.

— Watching people while they are eating
— Using a handkerchief in public
— Eating with your left hand
— Keeping your shoes on in another person's house
— Smoking in a person's home without asking permission
— Using a person's first name when you've just met them
— Starting to eat without saying anything to wish people a good meal
— Not answering an invitation
— Letting a door swing in someone's face
— Making remarks about a person's appearance or accent
— Asking how much someone earns
— ....
— ....

In small groups, compare your ideas. How important do you think that any of the above items are? List the ones you consider unimportant.

In your country, are there different codes of politeness:

— for children and for adults?
— for men and for women?

Are codes of politeness in a society important? Or do they just encourage people to be hypocritical?

2 People can be very rude . . .

Can anyone in your group or class remember an occasion when someone was rude to them? For example:

– has an employee in a shop, a bank, or a post office ever been abrupt or unhelpful for some reason?
– have you ever made a mistake in traffic and found that drivers got very angry and rude? Or have other people who made mistakes become rude?
– Have you ever been treated impatiently when you were struggling with the language or customs in a different country?

Tell your stories to the other students.
Listeners: Discuss each story you heard, considering these two points:

– the possible cause for the person's rudeness
– the right way to cope with such rudeness

3 Talking rubbish or gibberish, or just dim-witted?

You are going to listen to two women telling stories about people being rude.

Look at these sentences first:

— She was working in Edinburgh and had rented ....
— She took an Indian cloth print to a shop to ....
— Every night she took a taxi home but one night she was persuaded to ....
— The shop assistant couldn't understand the mother's ....
— She couldn't understand the driver's ....
— The shop assistant spoke in the way she would to someone who was deaf or

 ....
— When she couldn't understand, he got irritated and ....
— She was downright rude, saying the cloth print would have to be ....
— Finally, he turned the destination light out and ....

▭ Work with a partner. Each of you should take notes on one of the two
stories. Listen to the tape. Decide which sentences go with which story, and
complete each sentence.

Work with another pair of students and talk about these questions:

— What caused the rudeness in these stories?
— Is one story more upsetting than the other?
— Are regional accents important in your country? Are people rude about
  them? How do people react to foreign accents?

15

4 Are young people getting ruder?

Quite often older people feel that the younger generation is less polite than they were. Are young people really getting ruder? What do you think?

Do other people in the class agree with you? If there is a division of opinion in the class, try to think of at least one or two specific examples which support your view. Take it in turns to present your point of view – politely! What do you think the causes could be? Is it worth trying to do something about it? What should be done?

Organise a local survey to discover whether people in your town or city think young people are getting ruder.

Each person in the class must ask at least three or four other people this question: 'Are young people (under 35) ruder than their elders?' Ask at least one or two people under 35, and the same number of people over 35. (Translate the question into your own language if you need to.)

Next class: Together, discuss the total results of your surveys. Can you draw a class graph to show the results visually? Is there a majority opinion revealed by the survey? Is it the same opinion as the majority in your class?

5 | All in a day's work

Daily routines at work and at home

1 My best time of day

	Monday	Tuesday	Wednesday	Thursday	Friday	Saturday	Sunday
8							
9							
10							
11							
12							
1							
2							
3							
4							
5							
6							
7							
8							

Think back over the last week. Think of as many things as you can that you enjoyed doing during that week, and write them into the appropriate slot of the weekly planner.

Are most of the activities you enjoyed connected with your work or your social life? Are most of them in one section of the weekly planner, e.g. in the evenings? What do you think this shows about your personality? Are you a 'morning person' or an 'evening person'? What about other members of your family?

Compare and talk about your planners with other students.

2 Routines, routines

Four people were asked to note down their work routines. They are: a solicitor, the director of a small language teaching company, an adult who has gone back to university to do a degree, and the stage manager of a theatre. Which person made which comment?

Compare your views with other students and justify your guesses.

1 The beginning of the day is pretty standard - I check the answerphone and the fax for messages. And of course I check my diary for the day. I make sure that everything, all my records and things, are up to date. You have to get rid of the backlog before starting the new day! But the rest of the day is much more chaotic, I never really know what's going to turn up. Sometimes I don't have any lunch at all.

2 Well the very first thing is — I just have to have a cup of coffee from the machine. And I usually see other people there, so we have a chat. Then if I've got a few minutes, I'll run over to the library and look up some of the material I need for the day. Then there are classes, of course. I always have lunch in the coffee bar with some friends, then I find a quiet spot to read or write up my notes for the next day.

3 As soon as I arrive, I have a cup of tea — but after that I can't say. It depends. I don't have any routine at all, I don't have that kind of job.

4 When I get in, the correspondence is on my desk, with the relevant files, and a cup of coffee — I've got a wonderful secretary! I deal with the letters, see clients, phone people. My lunch time is from one o'clock to two fifteen.

In your group, discuss these questions:

– Which of these jobs seems most attractive to you?
– Do you prefer to have daily, weekly or monthly routines?
– When you are studying, do you have a routine?
– Would you prefer an occupation with a lot of routine or a lot of variety?
– Are routines helpful at work? Why or why not?
– Do you prefer working with people who stick to their routines or with people who have no routines at all?

3 Keeping track . . . and keeping records

Do you have a way of planning your work life? And what about your social life? How effective is your way? Do you use any of the methods illustrated? Compare your practice with other students in the class.
If you don't plan very much: Have you ever been in amusing or embarrassing situations as a result?

Most workplaces have ways of keeping records. What about your private life? Which of the following ways do you use to help you remember what happened to you in the past? Add other ways if you wish, then choose the three that are most important to you.

- Keeping old things, e.g. baby clothes, old furniture
- Keeping newspaper clippings
- Collecting mementos, e.g. bus tickets, travel brochures, labels from food and drink, tickets or programmes from sporting events, films and plays
- Photo albums
- ....
- ....

Compare your choices with other students, and talk about any advantages or disadvantages involved.

4 My day

In the past, people kept written diaries as a daily record of their lives, either for themselves or for posterity. Nowadays, because everyone is so busy, people sometimes dictate a record of important days onto cassettes rather than writing.

▭ Listen to two people's recordings. The first is an aspiring actor, the second is the wife of a rock star who became famous after he left what was then the Soviet Union.

Work with a partner. Each of you should concentrate on one of the stories and take notes.

Work with another pair of students and check the details. Re-tell what happened on the two important occasions.

Record your reactions to the stories and to this way of preserving them, on tape.

Prepare notes for a spoken diary entry for one of these days:

- an important day that you remember from your life
- an imaginary day that you would like to think will happen to you in the future. What would your most exciting day be like?

In small groups, use your notes to tell each other about the day you chose. If it is possible, you could record the entries and play them to each other. *Listeners*: Comment and ask questions about the spoken diaries.

Do you think this method of remembering events will become more popular in the future?

6 | Getting away from it all

Opting out of a conventional lifestyle

1 An impossible dream?

Would you like to change your lifestyle?
Does the lifestyle in any of these photos
appeal to you?

⫸→

Look at these statements. Tick the ones that apply to yourself.

1 I travel more than fifteen minutes to get to work every day.
2 My job is O.K. but I'd like to be able to make more of my own decisions.
3 My job is O.K. but is not likely to change much over the next few years.
4 I don't see my colleagues outside work.
5 I would say there is a lot of pressure in my life.
6 I feel that if I had more money, life would be easier.
7 I feel that my city, town or village is too crowded.
8 I feel that my city, town or village is rather dangerous.
9 I want to be closer to nature.
10 I don't like the present political climate in the country where I live.
11 I'm tired of the job I'm doing.
12 I'm bored with the routine of my life.
13 I need more challenge in my life, something to test the kind of person I am.
14 I need more personal space to develop my own personality.
15 I'd really like a more adventurous life.

Calculate your score. Look at sentences 1–10 and give yourself one point for each tick; then look at sentences 11–15 and give yourself two points for each tick.

With two or three other students, compare your scores. In your group, discuss and write the advice you would give to people who have scored as follows:

Scores:
0–7:   You seem quite content with your life. Our advice is
         ....
8–14:   You seem not entirely content with your present life. Our
         advice is ....
15–20: You must be extremely restless! Our advice is
         ....

Work with another group. Look at each person's score, and give your group's advice for that score. (If your class is large, you can do this several times.)

2 It's one thing to dream about it, but could we really do it?

Imagine that you have opted out of your present society and decided to try an alternative lifestyle. Look at the photos and choose an environment in which you would like to live.

→→→→→

Work with two or three other students who have chosen the same environment. Imagine that you have opted out together. Discuss the following options and try to agree on your choices, if at all possible.

1 Choose a house:

2 Choose the number of companions you want to take with you:
   a) 0   b) 1–3   c) 4–9   d) 10–20   e) over 20
3 Choose the social organisation you want to adopt:
   a) none   b) one leader, elected by the rest   c) a ruling committee with no leader   d) other: ....
4 Choose the ways you are going to subsist:
   a) hunting/fishing   b) growing your own food   c) making things and selling them   d) living from charity or donations from sponsors
   e) living from welfare payments from the state   f) other:

   ....

5 Briefly discuss any problems that you think might arise and how you would resolve them. For example, would you be able to cope with medical problems? What would happen if a member of the community broke your rules?

When the discussion time is up, consider these questions:

– Were you able to agree easily?
– Which choices proved the most difficult?
– Did any of you feel you would really be able to opt out in this way?

Organise feedback from the various groups to the class. Report on your discussion and the answers to the three questions.

3 They talked about it . . .

📼 Listen to two people talking about the way in which they would like to opt out. Make notes to answer these questions:

Speaker 1: What kind of lifestyle does he talk about? Why does it appeal to him?
Speaker 2: What kind of lifestyle does she talk about? Why does it appeal to her? Can she see any disadvantages?

Do you agree with either of the speakers?

4 She really did it!

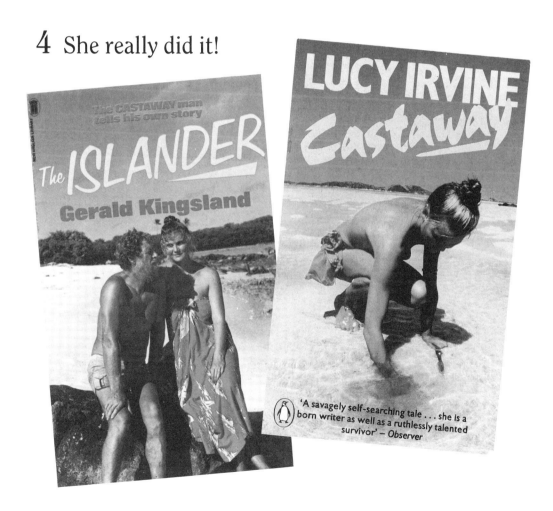

In the 1970s, Lucy Irvine answered this advertisement in a newspaper:

Writer seeks 'wife' for year on tropical island

She went off to live with a stranger on an island, for the period of one year.

⋙→

Imagine that you have seen a similar advertisement:

Writer seeks companion for year on tropical island

You can choose to imagine that the writer is a man or a woman.
Think about these questions:

— How would your family and friends react?
— What would be your main fears about the whole thing?
— What would you be looking forward to most?

Compare your thoughts on these questions with other students.

These are some of the problems that Lucy Irvine encountered during her stay on the island:

— running out of water
— not having enough to eat
— eating poisonous fruit
— storms
— frequently developing ulcers and sores
— often feeling she couldn't stand her companion

In small groups, discuss these problems. How would you have coped with them in her situation? Are any of her problems similar to ones you might have had in the alternative lifestyle you chose in activity 2? What would be the main learning experiences to be derived from a challenge of this kind? Talk about ways in which the experience might help you to develop and grow as a person.

Now that you've thought and talked about opting out, what do you really think about it? Is it a good idea? Or is it a bad idea?

7 | Remember, remember

Memory and memory failures

1 I can remember faces, but . . .

Complete these two unfinished sentences.

I find it easy to remember ....

I find it hard to remember ....

Work with two or three other students and discuss each other's sentences. Talk about problems you have remembering different things.

Find out what the majority of people in the class find most difficult to remember. How many of you think you have fairly good memories? Do some of you have selective memories, i.e. you can remember some things and not others?

Now try this simple test. Write down everything you can remember about the street just in front of the school. (Don't look out of the windows if you can see it!) Are there any trees? How many? Are there any street signs, fences, railings, shops, etc?

Which of you can produce the greatest number of details?

2 I'm so embarrassed when I forget someone's name

[cassette icon] Listen to a conversation between three friends. Note down as many details as you can to show what each one is good or bad at.

	Good at remembering	*Bad at remembering*
Speaker 1		
Speaker 2		
Speaker 3		

Check your details with other students. Do you have similar views to those of the speakers?

Do you think your memory is getting worse as you grow older? Can you explain this? Do you think it's inevitable?

3 Mnemonics

Do you have any mnemonics, i.e. special ways of remembering things? For example, how do you try to remember:

– phone numbers?
– the names of people you meet?
– things that you are supposed to be doing later?

Compare your methods with other students in the class.

Here are some well-known memory aids. Which ones are similar to the methods you discussed?

1 Using something physical to remind yourself, e.g. a string around your finger

2 Writing notes to yourself and leaving them in visible places

3 Concentrating very hard on the thing you want to remember. For example, trying to visualise its shape and colours, giving abstract things, e.g. numbers, a special shape and colour and concentrating on that

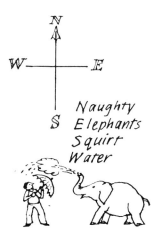

4 Associating each item with something that rhymes with it. For example, to memorise the number 5784, visualise a bee hive in a blue heaven, beside an iron gate leading to a red door

5 Writing a note on the back of your hand if all else fails

4 To remember an English word, I . . .

Learning a language involves a lot of memory work. What do you do to remember words in English?

With a partner, discuss the following methods.

1 Visual association. Associate each word with a specific visual image. Write the words in a pleasing pattern on a large piece of paper and beside each, make a simple line drawing showing the visual image with which it is associated (or paste a picture you have cut out from a magazine). Re-read the words several times, concentrating on the visual image each time.
2 Contextualising. For each word, write an English sentence or two in which the word is used appropriately. Re-read the sentences several times.
3 Translation and re-reading. Write the words in a list, with the translation into your own language beside each one. Repeat the list out loud several times.
4 Similar sounds. Write the words in a list. Next to each one, write a word which has a similar sound in your own language (even if it does not mean the same thing). Repeat the list, and try to associate the English word with the similar-sounding word in your own language.
5 Your own. Describe your own method if it is not in this list.

Your teacher will now give you a list of words to learn. Use any method that you like. After a few minutes, see how many of the words you can remember.

Organise class feedback and find out how many methods were actually tried. How many were considered successful?

Optional extension: Let a week pass. Put away your written lists and do not look at them during that week. After a week, see how many of the words you can remember. Work with two other people and give a short report on the method you used, how you felt about it, and whether you thought it was successful.

5 The storehouse of memory

Memory has been described as one of the greatest sources of continuing pleasure and joy. Think of a special moment in your life, one that you would like to remember and talk about. Try to visualise the scene again. Make brief notes under these headings:

— where the scene takes place
— when it takes place – morning, afternoon, or evening
— who else is there with you
— the main colours you can see around you
— what you can smell
— what you can hear
— what is your mood

Work with another student and describe your special moment to each other.

With a partner, read this simple poem and share your reactions to it.

One for the storehouse

The fading evening light;
Your face
deeply engrossed
in a book;
The stillness
and the noise
of the sea;
All this,
will I put
in my storehouse
of good memories.
And hold it
against the coming storms.

Meiling Jin, *Gifts from my grandmother*

Optional follow-up: Use your notes to create a poem of your own, or a poster that shows the visual aspects of your special memory.

8 | My brilliant career?

Ambition, jobs and career counselling

1 Do I really want all that pressure?

How ambitious are you? Would you like to get to the top of your job or career? With a partner, discuss arguments for and against ambition and list ways of completing these sentences.

I want to get to the top because ....
I don't want to get to the top because ....

Work with another pair of students and talk about your lists and your own ambitions.

2 The ladder of success

Work in small groups. Think of a successful person you admire and tell the other people in the group about the life of the person without saying who it is. Can they guess who you are thinking of?

What are the main factors in the success of these people? What are the main rungs in their 'ladder of success'? Discuss other factors you would put on the ladder.

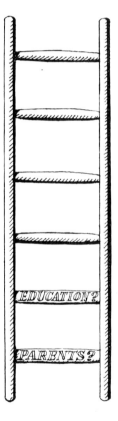

Draw one of these ladders for yourself:

a) a job ladder
   Put the jobs you have had on different rungs. Create rungs for jobs or positions you hope to have in the future.
b) a personal development ladder
   Put any past or current development on the rungs (the development of a skill, e.g. learning English, or things like establishing a home, raising children). Continue the ladder's rungs beyond the present to show what you hope to achieve in the future.

With another student, compare ladders and talk about your jobs or personal development landmarks to date, and your hopes for the future.

3 Careers advice

What advice did you receive about the choice of a career? Who advised you? Was it your parents, your school, your friends, or a professional career guidance service?

Was the advice you received useful, in your opinion? Tell another student about your experiences with career advice. Who is the best person to give such advice?

📼 On the cassette there are two conversations in which people discuss advice on careers. Work with your partner.

Partner A: Listen and take notes on the first conversation:

– What kind of advice does Judy's husband give young people?
– Who gave advice to Judy's daughter? Was it good advice?
– What kind of advice did Judy herself get as a young girl?

Partner B: Listen and take notes on the second conversation:

– What kind of advice did Nick receive at school?
– Did it help with the decisions he had to make?
– Who gave Janine the best advice? What was it?

When you have taken notes, join your partner and another pair of students. Tell each other about the conversations you heard.

Do any of the speakers relate experiences which were similar to your own? What do you think of the views they express?

4 Creating a questionnaire about careers

Imagine that you want to advise teenagers in your locality about possible careers. You want to help them discover occupations which best suit them individually.

Step 1   Creating a questionnaire
In small groups, create a questionnaire to find out what each teenager is really looking for in a job. Consider these and other factors:

— a large salary
— rapid promotion
— security
— interesting and varied work
— helping other people
— ....
— ....

Pin up all the group questionnaires so that you can read and discuss other people's ideas.

Optional project extension: If you like, you can continue this activity as a class project.

Step 2   Researching job opportunities
Each group in the class chooses one job category, for example:

— jobs related to environmental protection
— working for travel companies
— teaching English or another language
— working in a sports organisation
— doing community work with the elderly
— working in health care
— working with international aid organisations
— other types of occupation in your area: ....

When you have chosen your category, find out:

— What jobs are available?
— What qualifications are needed?
— What personal qualities are needed?
— What are the promotion prospects?

Collect brochures, pamphlets, articles, or any other relevant information.

Step 3   Feedback
Each group presents the information it has found, and displays its brochures or pamphlets, for example by creating posters.

As a class, discuss the results. Are there good job opportunities in your area?

Your Careers Service can help you right through sixth form and college

We can give you information and advice about:

- ▷ choosing a career
- ▷ job opportunities in your chosen field
- ▷ courses in further and higher education
- ▷ training programmes
- ▷ entry requirements
- ▷ how to apply for jobs, training and courses

Exam results not as good as you hoped?

The Careers Service can help you to find universities, polytechnics and colleges which may accept you.

We can advise you about alternatives, such as retakes, training schemes and jobs.

Or are they better than you expected?

We can help you with late applications to further and higher education courses.

Careers Officers regularly visit schools and colleges to help students.
Some colleges have a careers office on site.
You can also visit your local careers office for help and advice.

Your careers office is open all the year round, even during school and college holidays.
Don't leave it until the last minute.
The earlier you act the more help we can give you.

If you are a student in higher education you may have your own appointments board or advisory service.

However you can still use your Careers Service if you wish.

**Please keep in touch with us.
If the address of our local office is not on the back of this leaflet look in the Phone Book for 'Careers Service' or under your local education authority.**

35

9 | Magic moments

Magic and legends from the past or the present

1 Special objects

Do you know what these objects are or were used for? With another student, choose one object with which you are not familiar and try to guess:

— Who used the object?
— Where?
— For what purpose?

Check your guesses and compare your ideas with other students in the class.

Are there any objects in your own country which are used today or were used in the past for particular ceremonies or for healing? Describe them to other students in the class.

2 Magic symbols

Complete this sentence in any way that shows what you think.

For me, the word 'magic' implies ....

Compare your sentences with other students in the class, and talk about your views. Does magic still have a meaning in our modern 'scientific' world? Is belief in magic something that adults grow out of? Or can it be a valuable source of fantasy and imagination? Can you think of any stories about magic you believed when you were a child? What do you think of them now?

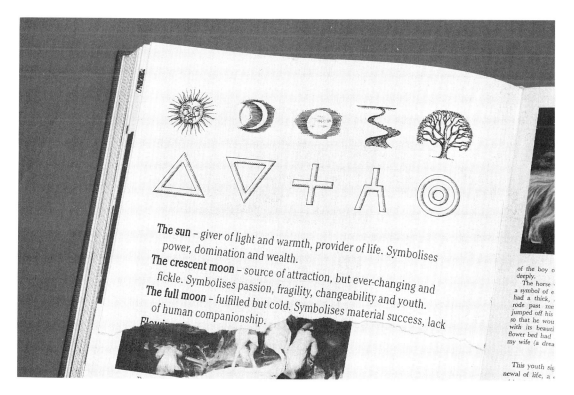

The sun – giver of light and warmth, provider of life. Symbolises power, domination and wealth.

The crescent moon – source of attraction, but ever-changing and fickle. Symbolises passion, fragility, changeability and youth.

The full moon – fulfilled but cold. Symbolises material success, lack of human companionship.

of the boy o
deeply.
The horse
a symbol of e
had a thick,
rode past me
jumped off his
so that he wou
with its beauti
flower bed had
my wife (a drea

This youth si
newal of life, a

3 Hundreds of years ago, in the twentieth century . . .

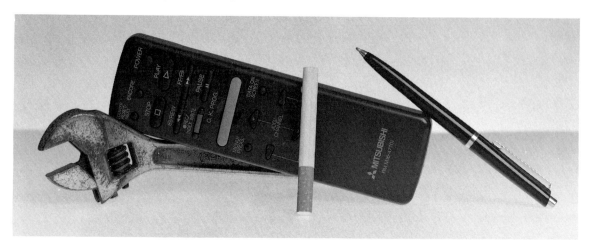

With another student, imagine that one object from your everyday life has survived a catastrophic destruction of our present civilisation. Choose one of the objects in the photos or decide on one of your own.

Imagine that you are scientists who find the object many hundreds of years later. You decide that it must have been some kind of magic object used for special rituals in that far-off past, the twentieth century.

Prepare a presentation for other scientists in which you:

– describe the physical appearance of the strange object
– say what rituals you think it was used for
– say what you think it indicates about the long-lost civilization

Listeners: Can you guess the object found?

Which description was the most convincing? Which was the most amusing?

SOUTHWESTERN REGION NUMBER THREE, MUSEUM OF ANTIQUITIES

Exhibit A208.2: *tip of ritual wand, probably late 20th Century AD – fine paper tightly rolled, pungent herbal substance filling, flattened gold hinge probably used as joining mechanism to main ceremonial helmet or weapon. Traces of incineration still visible on the lateral extremity have led to speculation about its function in fire ceremonies, or possibly hallucinatory appeasement sacrifices, a hypothesis reinforced by discoveries of several collections of similar wands carefully deposited in folded positions in glass or metal ornamental cases.*

4 Once upon a time . . .

Many countries have folk tales or very old legends in which some form of magic plays an important part. Can you think of any from your own country?

Here are two stories of this kind, the first from Australia, the second from Africa. The endings are missing.
With your partner, read the beginnings of the two stories, choose one of them and prepare an ending for it.

1

HOW SPENCER GULF WAS CREATED

Spencer Gulf, in South Australia, was once a valley filled with a line of fresh-water lagoons, stretching northwards for a hundred miles or more. Each lagoon was the exclusive territory of a species of water bird – swans, ducks or water hens. The trees belonged to the eagles, crows and parrots, while in the open country lived emus, dingoes, kangaroos, snakes, and lizards.

For a long time all lived in harmony. But trouble started when the birds, because of their greater numbers, more beautiful appearance, and their ability to fly, felt so superior to the rest of creation that they prohibited the animals and reptiles from drinking at the lagoons. And so a long conflict began in which many were killed, and land-dwellers died of thirst.

In those days the kangaroo was a man who was sad because of the unnecessary fighting. He thought and thought about how he could possibly end it.

2   A MAN WITH A TREE GROWING OUT OF HIS HEAD

One day a man who had never done anything wrong noticed that a tree was growing out of his head. This was not painful to the man, but made him feel awkward when other people were around. He asked his wife to chop down the tree, but she was afraid that he might bleed to death if she did. So instead he went to see a woman who could use charms to solve difficult problems. She lived in a hut some distance away and so the man had to bear the stares of all the people as he walked to her place.

The charm woman said he must have done something bad to have this happen, but the man insisted that he had always behaved well. In that case, said the woman, he must be planning to do something bad. She took a special herb out of her bag and said he must eat it every day for a week. He must also pay her two cows, for the herb was expensive and it was not easy to stop trees growing out of people's heads. The man promised to do that.

When everyone is ready, tell your story to another pair of students. Decide whether the story has a moral. What is it?

When you have all told your stories, you can find the original endings in the Key. As a class, try to supply a moral for each tale. Do the legends, as you wrote them, have different morals from the originals?

10 | Threatening times

Dangers for individuals, countries, the planet

1 The biggest threat to our natural environment is . . . unbridled tourism

Think about your own country. With a partner, choose two of the shapes and discuss what you consider the main threats to that particular aspect of life in your own country. Note down a few ideas for each aspect.

Compare your diagrams with other students and see if you can build up a complete set.

If you had to nominate the biggest threat for your country, which would you choose? Compare and explain your views.

2 The biggest threat to the planet is . . . unbridled industrialisation

What about the planet? Talk about these issues:

— Do you think these are threatening times for the world as a whole?
— What are the main dangers, in your opinion?
— Are you optimistic or pessimistic about the planet's future? Why?

You are going to listen to three people discussing their views on the biggest threat to the planet. These are the things they talk about. Before you listen, look at the gapped list.

Speaker 1: global .... ; the felling of the .... ; the upsetting of the .... ; the hole in the ....

Speaker 2: an .... catastrophe; a .... catastrophe; World ....

Speaker 3: nuclear .... ; the ozone .... ; the collecting of .... ; the .... of waste; moves made by the scientific community, ... government and .... government.

▣ Listen to the three speakers and fill in the blanks. Are the speakers optimistic or pessimistic about the planet?

Are you worried about any of the same things? Did the speakers say anything you did not agree with? Compare your reactions with other students in the class.

3 Small steps for individuals or groups

Discuss these questions.

1 Who is responsible for dealing with the threatening aspects that you have talked about, either in your own country or in the world?
2 Is there anything that individuals or groups can do about them?
3 What ways are there of putting pressure on governments or industry so that action is taken? Are any of the following likely to be effective? (You can suggest your own ways if you wish.)
   – publicity campaigns, e.g. billboards, newspapers, radio, television
   – petitions presented to the authorities
   – demonstrations, e.g. marches, sit-ins
   – ....
   – ....

⋙→

How do you feel? Choose one of these responses:

A: Individuals should be concerned about threats to their country or the world, and try to do something about them.
B: Individuals needn't be concerned. It may be better to leave these matters to the experts.

Work with two or three other students who share your opinion.

Group A: Choose one of the threatening aspects you identified earlier. Discuss the best ways of planning a campaign against it. Decide on the action to be taken. If it is likely to be expensive, think of ways in which your group could raise money.
Group B: Distribute yourselves among the A groups. Join the discussion and try to present arguments against the planned campaign.

When you are ready, work with students from other groups and explain to each other the situation that you looked at and how you decided to respond to it.

Organise class feedback and pool your ideas. Which strategies that you heard about would be most effective? Are there any which you would really like to carry out? How much influence do pressure groups really have in your country? Have any of your views changed since you started this unit?

11 | Love, hope and charity

Charity appeals

1 My first priority

SAVE THE NORTH SEA

THE NORTH SEA – AN ENVIRONMENT UNDER THREAT.

DOLPHIN KILLER

This is a single strand of netting like that used by the drift net fishermen. It looks quite soft and flimsy. But pull it and you'll find it surprisingly strong. And when woven into miles and miles of netting, this flimsy nylon thread becomes the 'wall of death' which traps and kills over a hundred helpless dolphins every hour. That's because like us, dolphins breathe air. And so once entangled in the fishermen's net, these sensitive creatures slowly drown.

For centuries the countries bordering the North Sea have used it as their dustbin into which they have tipped chemical wastes and sewage. When not using the sea as a dustbin they continue to exploit its resources through overfishing and oil and mineral extraction. We are now beginning to see the effects of this abuse...

■ A viral epidemic (possibly originating in sewage effluent) killed more than 17,000 seals in the North Sea in 1988.

■ Toxic algal blooms have contaminated shellfish populations around our coasts, causing the closure of many fisheries. These algae thrive in nutrient rich seas. Eutrophication of the seas is in part caused by modern day farming techniques.

■ Bathing in the sea off Britain's beaches can cause upset stomachs and skin rashes. These problems are caused by bacteria found in sewage and sewage effluent. The U.K. is presently pumping 300 million gallons of sewage and sewage effluent into our coastal waters daily.

■ In the Orkneys and Shetland Isles major seabird colonies are failing to breed. This breeding failure could be due to diminishing fish populations as we continue to take an unsustainable portion of those fish still living in the North Sea.

Do you support any charities? If so, which ones and why? If not, why not?
With a partner, discuss your answers and opinions.

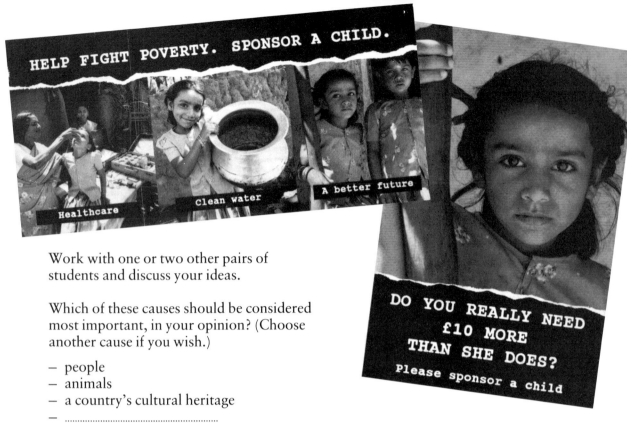

HELP FIGHT POVERTY. SPONSOR A CHILD.

Healthcare

Clean water

A better future

DO YOU REALLY NEED
£10 MORE
THAN SHE DOES?
Please sponsor a child

Work with one or two other pairs of students and discuss your ideas.

Which of these causes should be considered most important, in your opinion? (Choose another cause if you wish.)

– people
– animals
– a country's cultural heritage
– ....

Work with two or three other students who have chosen the same cause. In your group, list as many charities as you can for this cause. Choose three charities that you consider should be at the top of the list.

Compare your views with other groups.

2 We'd like to feel we're doing something positive

In your groups, think of a charity you do support, or might be willing to support. Discuss these questions:

1 What are the best ways of supporting the charity? What can you realistically do yourselves?
2 What would be the best ways of raising funds in your own area?
3 What would you especially want to say to people to get their support?
4 What drawbacks or problems can you imagine?
5 How can you ensure that aid actually reaches the problem?

🔲 Listen to two people speaking about their favourite charity. Divide your group in two. Half the group should take notes on the first speaker and the other half should take notes on the second speaker.

When you are ready, check your notes with other students in your half of the group. Then work with a partner from the other half of the group. Tell each other what the speaker's views were and compare them with your own.

3 A commercial

Work with two other students. Imagine that you are going to create a short radio or television commercial to raise funds for charity. Decide which of these formats is the best to use:

— one person making an appeal, e.g. a famous person
— a mixture of talk and pictures showing the needy
— a presentation with songs or music
— other: ....

Discuss the language and persuasion techniques that you will need.

Prepare the commercial. If you like, find pictures or music to accompany your commercial. Rehearse the roles you are going to play in the commercial.

Present your commercial to the class.
Listeners: Make notes on the aspects of the presentations you particularly like, and discuss them afterwards. How effective were the commercials?

4 Mini-debate on charities (Optional extension)

Organise an informal mini-debate in your class. (If your class is large, divide it into two groups. Each group should prepare a mini-debate on one subject and present it in front of the other group.)

First of all, choose a subject (in debates, called the 'motion') that is likely to be controversial in your class. Choose one of these motions or one of your own:

— We have a duty to help people who are less well-off than we are.
— Our country has a duty to give aid to countries that are less well-off.
— Giving charity is degrading to the people who receive it.
— ....

Form two teams, those who support the motion and those who are against it. In your team, prepare arguments to support your side. Try to anticipate the arguments that the other team is likely to use, and think of ways of countering them.

When you are ready, elect one person from each side to chair the debate jointly. If you can, sit in a circle, or in two lines with opposing sides facing each other. Each person on the team has the chance to make a speech of not more than two minutes. When that person has spoken, someone from the opposing side is given a chance to present contrary arguments.

When everyone has made a presentation, the floor is open to anyone who wishes to make further points or continue the debate.

12 | Buildings to look at and to work in

Good and bad features of public buildings

1 Old or new?

With a partner, discuss these questions about the city, town or village in which you are now living:

- Are there any old buildings?
- Can you describe them?
- Are there any new buildings?
- Can you describe them?
- Do you prefer old buildings or new buildings? Can you say why?

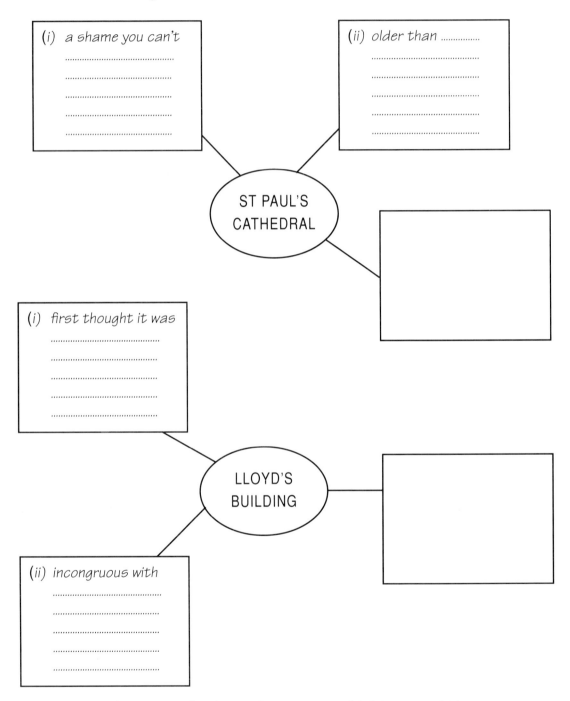

Listen to an American talking to friends about two buildings, one old and one new, in London. Complete the diagrams to show the comments made about the two buildings.

(i) a shame you can't

....

....

....

....

....

(ii) older than ....

....

....

....

....

....

ST PAUL'S
CATHEDRAL

(i) first thought it was

....

....

....

....

....

LLOYD'S
BUILDING

(ii) incongruous with

....

....

....

....

....

Compare your diagrams with other students. Do you think it's a good idea to have a mixture of old and new buildings in a city?

2 Good and bad public buildings

With another student, think again about your city, town or village.

– Choose one public building in it that you like: ....
  Why do you like it? List as many good features as you can. Does it have
  any drawbacks?
– Choose one public building in it that you dislike: ....
  Why do you dislike it? List as many bad features as you can. Does it have
  any redeeming features?

Organise class feedback and compare the buildings you chose. Discuss the
reasons for your choice. Is there general agreement in your class?

3 Different people, different views . . .

⊡ Listen to a conversation between four people talking about buildings they like or dislike. Two people agree on a building they like a lot, the Van Gogh museum in Amsterdam, while the other two disagree about a war memorial church in Berlin.

Work with a partner. One of you should take notes on the good features of the Van Gogh museum and the other should take notes on the features of the Berlin church considered good or bad.

Check your notes with another pair of students. Do you know the buildings the speakers are talking about? If you do not, can you imagine them quite clearly, or not?

4 Role play: buildings to work in (Optional extension)

This is a role play or game of persuasion, for groups of four or six people.
Work in two teams, each of two or three students.

1 Preparing the grids

GRID A **Kinds of workplace**

a doctor's surgery		secretarial offices
	an artist's studio	
a small shop		a classroom for a private language school

GRID B **Features of the workplace**

right next to a major motorway		large windows facing north
	very thin walls inside	
views over the fields to the mountains		low ceilings and few windows

In your team, copy these two grids onto a piece of paper, and complete them.
Fill in the squares of grid A with different kinds of workplaces. Fill in the
squares of grid B with either positive or negative features of any office space.

When your grids are complete, number the squares in grid A from 1 to 9, in a
random fashion. Use letters from A to L to label the squares in grid B, again
in a random fashion. Do not show your grids to the opposing team.
When you are ready, join the other team.

2 Choosing

Each person in the group will choose one number from 1–9 and three letters
from A–L. The students in the other team will tell you the workplace and the
three features you have chosen from their grid.

3 Preparing

You will now have five minutes' preparation time. You are going to play the
role of estate agents, trying to rent the workplace you have been given, with
its three main features, to a prospective buyer. Discuss the problems with
other students in your team.

4 Persuading

Take it in turns to play the role of the estate agent, trying to rent the
workplace. Make sure you mention all three features, emphasising any good
features, and disguising or minimising the effects of any bad features. One
person from the other team is the prospective buyer.

13 | Buildings to live in

Homes, present and future

1 A room of one's own

With a partner, discuss the words you would use to describe these rooms. Which do you prefer? To what extent do you think you can tell a person's personality from their room? How important is your home to you? Do you like to have one room at least that reflects your personality? Or are you someone who could live happily anywhere?

2 One of the loveliest rooms I've ever been in

Think about a room that you really like either in your own home or someone else's house or flat. What do you especially like in it? Consider these features:

- the colours, e.g. pale and restful, bright and exciting, dark and mysterious
- the windows, e.g. small, pretty, large, arched
- the furniture and furnishings (What are they like?)
- the way the room is arranged
- the room's general effect, e.g. restful, peaceful, exciting, vibrant, friendly

How do you feel when you are in that room? Talk about the room you chose with other students and ask questions about the room they chose.

▭ Listen to Marya talking about a house that she likes a lot, and her favourite room within it. As you listen, note down the features she particularly likes, and how she feels when she is in the room and why.

With a partner, check your answers and then compare your ideas on these two questions:

- What is your general impression of the room Marya describes?
- In what ways is it similar to or different from the room you described?

3 Home is where the heart is

What aspects are most important to you in a home? With a partner, look at this list, and choose the three factors which you consider most important for a successful home. Add other factors if you think important ones are missing.

- It should be situated near friendly neighbours or your family.
- It should have personal possessions which mean a lot to you.
- It should be in a quiet location.
- It should have an efficient kitchen.
- It should have an efficient bathroom.
- It should have good central heating/a good air conditioning system.
- It should be appropriate for its environment.
- It should have a comfortable sitting room.
- It should be near your work.
- It should be near shops.
- ....
- ....

Organise class feedback and find the three aspects that were chosen most often by members of your class. How many of these aspects are present in the traditional homes of the past in your region? How many are present in new homes in your region?

4 What will homes be like in the future?

What do you think homes will be like in the future? In small groups, discuss and describe the main features as you imagine them.

Prepare an advertisement or a poster about your ideal home of the future. Include information about:

— where the house is in relation to others
— the number of rooms
— the function of the rooms
— the main living area or room in the house (Draw a plan if you like.)

Organise an exhibition of ads or posters in your classroom. Circulate and ask questions about the houses.

Which house would you most like to rent for a month? Which houses were the most different from present day houses, in your opinion? Which were the most attractive? Which were the most horrifying?

14 The benefit of experience

Creating information guides and cassettes

This is a group project, which may stretch over two or three class periods. If you do not wish to devote so much time to project work, you might nevertheless enjoy doing activities 1, 2 and 3.

1 In our experience

In small groups, talk about the town or city where you are living. Consider these questions and try to add some others:

1 Where can you get good meals or snacks in your town or city that are not too expensive?
2 What can people do in their spare time?
3 What sports facilities are there?
4 Are there good places to buy books or clothes that are not too expensive?
5 How can you find pleasant accommodation that is not too expensive?
6 .... ?
7 .... ?

Make a list of the group's suggestions. Compare your suggestions with other groups. Are their ideas similar?

2 The best place to buy books is . . .

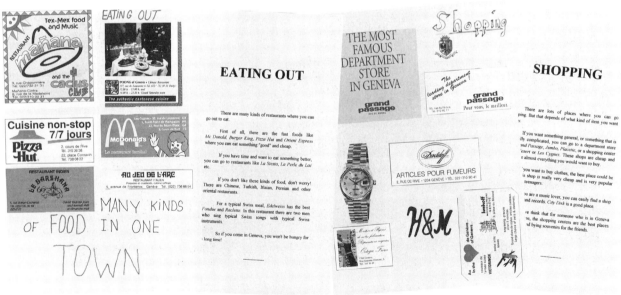

You are going to create an information pack, either to provide guidance to future students at your school, or for tourists or visitors to your town. An option is to record a cassette to accompany the pack.

Gather as much information about the town and its facilities as you can. Add details about any places mentioned, e.g. how to find them on the town map, specialities, the names of particularly welcoming staff, etc. Try to make sure your information is accurate, by phoning, checking with other groups, or, if you can, visiting the places on your list.

3 Pooling resources

When you are ready, prepare brief reports for the rest of the class about what you have discovered. Give up-to-date details on things like new prices, new owners, new premises, new facilities.

Take notes on the findings of other groups.

4 Producing the guides – Phase 1 Preparation

Prepare a first draft of guides and recording scripts. Different people like to work in different ways, but you might like to consider the following steps:

1 As a class, decide which group is going to prepare which section of the guide.
2 Decide what kind of guide and cassette you want to produce. Do you want it to be formal or informal, serious or chatty and light-hearted?
3 Choose one or two people to be editors. They will have to be prepared to help the different groups and co-ordinate the writing and recording.
4 Decide on target dates for completion of the first draft of each section, and the first draft of the script for the cassette.

5 Producing the guides – Phase 2 Revision and recording

When your first drafts and first scripts are completed, it is time to revise and record. The following steps might be useful:

1 With the help of your teacher, check the English in your guides and scripts. It might be useful for your group to let other students read them and say whether everything is clear and interesting.
2 Try to obtain good visuals, designs, maps, to make the guide visually attractive.
3 Record your cassette.
4 Finalise the layout of written sections and visuals.
5 Produce an index and contents page, if that is appropriate.
6 Arrange to have the booklet written out or typed as neatly as possible.

6 Class feedback

As a class, discuss the project you have just taken part in. Did you enjoy doing the project? Do you think the resulting guide would be useful for future students or visitors?

Here are the views of groups which have undertaken similar projects:

– Some think the resulting project is likely to be interesting and valuable for future generations of students.
– Others feel that the project will probably not be used very much, but that it had valuable side effects in creating group solidarity between the people who actually worked hard to make it a reality.

Do either of these two views coincide with your own?

15 Special cases?

Providing for different needs

1 Providing for different needs

With another student, consider the country in which you are now living.
What provisions are there to help people with special needs? List the ones
you think are most important.

Compare your views with other students. Are the provisions that exist
sufficient, in your opinion? Is anything important missing?

2 Education and training

What is the best education for young people with special needs? Which of the following groups do you think could benefit from special schools? Which groups should be educated in ordinary schools as much as possible?

Young people who are:

— in wheelchairs
— dyslexic
— deaf
— exceptionally intelligent
— blind

Young people who have:

— special talents, e.g. musical talents or other artistic gifts
— exceptional sporting ability
— a reading age much lower than their age group

Compare your views with other students and try to give reasons for them.

3 Case study: a conflict

Jane is a handicapped girl, aged 13, who is confined to a wheelchair. At her first school, she was with other children in an ordinary classroom, but now it is time for her to transfer to upper school. The local school says it will not accept her because it lacks facilities for wheelchairs. Jane and her parents would prefer her to remain with her friends.

Listen to taped interviews with some of the people involved in the dispute. Note down details about the attitudes of the various people interviewed, and the reasons they give.

People interviewed	Attitudes to the problem/reasons
1 Jane's mother	
2 A representative of the national association for the disabled	
3 A representative of the local authority	
4 A schoolfriend of Jane's	
5 The Principal of the local upper school	

Check the details with other students. What do you think of the speakers' views? Which speakers were:

— most reasonable?
— most convincing?

What are your own views on the problem?

4 Case study: solutions

Imagine that your group is the committee responsible for resolving Jane's case. Consider the following solutions, and choose one of them or one of your own:

1 Convince Jane and her parents that it is important for her to go to the special school for the disabled. Arrange for her to visit it so that she can see for herself how useful it would be for her to attend classes there.
2 Sell part of the school's playing fields to finance the building of the ramps and special toilet facilities that are needed for Jane to remain at the local school.
3 Have a big community drive to raise money in order to provide the facilities needed.
4 Convince central government to donate the funds needed to change the school.
5 ....

When you have agreed on a solution, present it to the whole class, and explain the reasons for your decision.

16 | In sickness . . .

Pain and disease

a terrible ache   feeling very stiff   incredible tight feeling
moaning with pain   the most incredible pain   a very hot instant pain
frequent little stabbing pains   burning and painful   deep blunt pain
rolling and writhing on the bed   a shooting and stabbing pain

1 It was the most awful pain!

How would you describe the problems shown in the pictures? Do you think
any of the expressions in the box are appropriate for them? Compare your
ideas with other students. Have you ever had any of these problems yourself?
What is the most painful thing you have ever experienced?

🔊 Listen to four people talking about the worst pain they have ever had. Note down what caused the pain in each case. How do the first two speakers describe their feelings when the pain ended?

Speaker 1: ....
Speaker 2: ....
Speaker 3: ....
Speaker 4: ....

Listen again and put the number of the speaker next to any expression that you hear them say.

Compare your answers with other students.

2 Bedside manners

With a partner, talk about these questions:

– How important do you consider preventive medicine to be? Should you consult a doctor only when you're ill, or is it useful to have a check up from time to time, even when you're generally healthy?
– How do you feel about seeing a doctor? What do you particularly like or dislike about it?
– What are the factors that are most important to you in choosing a doctor?
– Would you like to be a doctor? Which parts of the job do you think you might enjoy? Which parts would you find difficult?

Work with one or two other pairs of students. Imagine that you are going to present a radio or television programme entitled: 'What does the public really think about doctors?' One person is the 'roving reporter' interviewing the others, who are members of the public. Prepare your programmes.

In turn, perform your programmes for other students in the class, and talk about the views expressed.

3 A country's biggest killer . . .

Other ways to help your heart

Heart disease is Britain's biggest killer. Every year, it claims the lives of nearly 110,000 people under the age of 75 – that's more than one person every five minutes.

Taking regular exercise is just one of the vital ways of protecting your heart. These other ways are important too.

Don't smoke

Every year, at least 100,000 people are killed by smoking. For help and advice on giving up smoking, contact ASH (Action on Smoking and Health), 109 Gloucester Place, London W1H 3PH. Telephone: 071-935 3519.

Watch your weight

Being overweight puts you at greater risk of heart disease, high blood pressure and other health problems. If you think you need to lose weight, ask your doctor to recommend a suitable diet.

Two useful British Heart Foundation guides to losing weight entitled *So you want to lose weight* are available free of charge. There is one for men and one for women. They give details of tasty menus and advice on healthy eating. Also available is a useful *Trim the fat from your diet* wallchart.

Eat less fat, more fibre

Foods that are high in saturated fats (like dairy products, sausages, meat pies, hamburgers, cakes and biscuits) and fried foods increase the amount of cholesterol in your blood.

- Try to eat more chicken and fish instead of red meat.
- Grill your food rather than fry.
- Try to choose vegetable cooking oils that are labelled 'high in polyunsaturates', and low-fat spreads.

- Fill up on fibre-rich foods like wholemeal bread, potatoes, rice, pasta, fresh vegetables and fruit.

Have your blood pressure checked

High blood pressure can increase your risk of having a stroke or heart attack. Every adult should have their blood pressure checked every few years by their GP.

Cut down on alcohol

Heavy drinkers are twice as likely to die of heart disease as non-drinkers. Too much alcohol also increases your risk of other diseases such as cancer and liver disease.

A unit of alcohol is equivalent to half a pint of normal strength beer or lager, or a single pub measure of spirits, wine or sherry.

A safe measure for men is no more than 21 units of alcohol a week. For women, the limit is no more than 14 units a week. It is best to avoid alcohol binges and try to have at least two alcohol-free days a week.

Consider these questions:

- What is your own country's biggest killer?
- What are the killer's obvious or possible causes?
- What advice would you give on ways of preventing it?

Circulate in your classroom. Try to speak to as many of the other students as possible in the time available. Exchange views on the three questions.

Optional feedback: Work in groups of three or four, and tell each other what you found most interesting in what you heard as you went round the class.

4 Mental anguish or physical pain?

How sharper than a serpent's tooth it is
To have a thankless child!

Shakespeare, King Lear

Mental anguish is sometimes said to be as strong as physical pain. With a partner, read these six extracts from modern novels, all of them describing a moment of pain.

Decide whether the sensations described had a physical, a mental, or an emotional cause. What do you think the circumstances were in each case?

1   There I was, swimming as it were, up and up, away from myself – I could see myself lying there, it was in an underpass at Pimlico tube station actually – I could see this body lying there like a banana-skin someone had dropped – and there was I, moving away quite fast up a kind of tunnel – or funnel thing – and at the other end was a sort of opening and an indescribable light, ever so bright.

2   He would feel he couldn't move, couldn't breathe and he would wake up with his skin wet from effort... He felt sick to his stomach.

3   She gave a cry and, clinging to her husband, slipped to the ground... I was unnerved by hearing Mrs. Dempster, I had never heard an adult cry in pain before. The sound was terrible to me. Falling, she burst into nervous tears...

4   The pain tightened in her gut – this one made it hard to breathe... She felt the pain coming into the dark cloud of her present terror... The pain came again. It was a tight hard pain, so hard she could not have talked if she had wanted to.

5   ... I tossed and panted and groaned as if I were wrestling with a palpable demon... I got up but was suffering such extreme local discomfort that I could hardly get dressed. I started making tea, but its smell sickened me. I drank a little whisky in a glass of water and began to feel very ill. I could not stand still but wandered distractedly and rapidly about the flat rubbing against the furniture as a tiger in a cage endlessly brushes its bars. I had ceased groaning and was now *hissing*.

6   His palms were sweating, his forehead was wet and itching, he felt shivery, his voice was shaky and his heart was beating fast... He could feel sweat start to gather in the lines of his forehead and in his eyebrows. Soon it would roll down his nose, and then what?...

Compare your ideas with other students. Then check the answers in the Key. Have any of you had any experiences similar to those described? Do you think physical pain or mental anguish is worse? Why?

17 | ...And in health

Alternative methods of healing

1 Remedies for common ailments: what works for you?

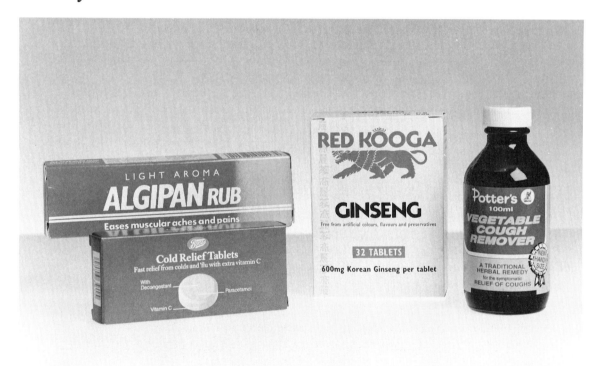

Do you know of any remedies that work for these common ailments? Add other ailments if you like.

— a common cold	— backache
— rashes	— a headache
— toothache	— muscle pain
—	— ....

Compare your ideas with other students. Do most people in your class rely on drugs, or do they use other methods?

2 Two anecdotes about alternative cures

Here are two anecdotes about cures that were not the result of medical treatment or drugs. Work with a partner. Each of you should read one of the anecdotes.

Anecdote A

My father was born at the beginning of the century, the ninth child in a family living in a poor area in rural Canada. Because he was the last child, he became the family's cosseted darling, the apple of my grandmother's eye. But he was a small, frail boy, and when only six he fell very seriously ill with an abdominal infection called peritonitis. The doctor told my grandmother that he would die. My grandmother drew herself to her full height, glared at the doctor and declared: 'He will not die.'

She harnessed their one horse to the little buggy, drove the eighty miles to the nearest town, and searched all the libraries for information about peritonitis. She returned triumphant. In distant Switzerland, an alternative healing method had been found to work in many cases. The whole family was set to work, fetching water from the pump and heating it on the big wood stove. The small child was repeatedly plunged into very hot water, then carried kicking and screaming out into the bitter cold to be rolled in the snow.

When the doctor was called back the following week, expecting to sign a death certificate, he was astounded to find a happy child playing by the fireside. 'It's a miracle!' he declared. 'But I'm sorry to have to warn you that his system has been terribly weakened. You cannot expect him to live for more than a few years at most.'

My grandmother glared at him again.

My father lived into his eighties, became a doctor himself, and, like the majority of his colleagues, was always extremely suspicious of alternative healing methods.

≫→

Anecdote B

The best present I ever received started as something of a joke. A cousin, a keen orientalist, brought me a pair of steel Healthy Balls from a journey around China. The balls are slightly smaller than billiard balls, lacquered in green, hand-painted with Siberian cranes and tree-covered crags, and contain a melodious chime.

Held in one hand, the balls are circulated first one way, then the other. The benefits of exercising the hands, particularly for old people, were apparently discovered during the Ming dynasty (14th–17th century).

At the time, although my cousin did not know it, I was suffering badly from RSI, or repetitive strain injury, in my hands and wrists. Every joint and tendon felt as though it was on fire.

I was under intense pressure to finish a book. But I was reduced to less than ten minutes' typing on the word processor at a time and then I would have to rest my hands for several hours.

At first, I found it almost impossible to rotate two balls, partly because of the cramped state of my hands, and partly due to an inherent lack of dexterity. Not until a physiotherapist suggested that I try manipulating the balls in a hot bath did it become easier. I began to notice a temporary easing of the worst symptoms.

Within a couple of days, the difference was so marked that I could work at the keyboard for up to 20 minutes at a time with relatively short breaks.

By the end of two weeks, the pain had gone, and I was able to work normally. If I went for a day or so without manipulating the balls, however, a little of the burning sensation would return and the tendons in my hands and wrists would start to tighten, although not as badly as before.

Tell your partner about the article you read. Then talk about it together. How many of the following do you think contributed to the cure in each case? Suggest other explanations if you can.

Anecdote A
- the 'alternative' method
- the grandmother's willpower
- the probability that the infection was healing and the child would have recovered in any case
- ....

Anecdote B
- the relaxing of muscles
- the stimulation of blood circulation
- the benefits of the hot bath
- ....

Does anyone in your class have similar anecdotes about unexpected or unorthodox cures for illness? Relate them to the class.

3 What is your experience of . . . ?

Reflexology &

Swedish Massage

For health, relaxation and stress management in your own home.

NADINE BAKER   390 4785

Massage

RELAXATION: to relieve stress and tension
SPORTS: both pre- and post-event
SHIATSU: acupressure for health and well-being

Claire Tsui
Massage Therapist
Hawthorn Physiotherapy Centre
Phone 0223 325521

YOU don't need a stress management course

- you're intelligent
- you're successful
- you've always coped
- you're too busy

But if that path is feeling rocky, timely expert help will have you back on track and enjoying life.

PSYCHOLOGY CONSULTANTS
Phone 373 5741

156 Courtnell Street, Hyde Park

REFLEXOLOGY

☆ The pure indulgence of having your feet massaged.
☆ The opportunity to escape from outside pressures.
☆ The chance to relax and liberate yourself from stress and anxiety.

332 4765 Kensington

Rediscover the joy of living

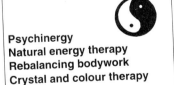

Psychinergy
Natural energy therapy
Rebalancing bodywork
Crystal and colour therapy

For appointment phone:
THE HOLISTIC HEALTH CENTRE
on 091 326 9002

Massage

We all need time to relax ...
Safe, non-sexual, therapeutic.

Anthony Davison
(071) 432 0232

What do you know about any of the methods shown in the advertisements? Have you tried any of them? Compare your experiences with other people in the class.

≫→

You are going to listen to four people talking about the various 'alternative' methods they have tried.

With a partner, listen to all four speakers. One person should take notes on Speakers 1 and 3, the other on Speakers 2 and 4. Try to note down information about:

— the problem the speaker was trying to resolve (if this is revealed)
— the methods the speaker tried
— what results these methods had
— the speaker's preferred method (if this is revealed)

Check your notes, then work with another pair of students. Tell each other the main ideas you noted from the recording.

4 I'd like to try . . . (Optional extension)

With one or two other students, choose an 'alternative medicine' method that you have tried or would like to try.

Try to find out as much as you can about this method by reading books or magazines, using libraries, interviewing practitioners, etc.

Prepare a visual (a brochure, an overhead transparency, slides, a poster, etc.) to show other students in the class the main points that you have found out.

Use your visual to help you make a short oral report to the class about your chosen method. Each of you should speak for about three or four minutes, and be prepared to answer questions from the class.

18 | Children and adults

Growing up, bringing up children

1 Memories

Are your dominant memories of your upbringing positive, negative or neutral? What is the earliest memory you have? Complete these sentences:

– I was brought up by ....
– I had .... brother(s), ...
  sister(s).
– The person I felt closest to as a young child was ....
– I think the person who had the strongest influence upon me as a child was
  ....
– The thing that I liked best about the way I was brought up was
  ....

Discuss your sentences with another student.

As a class, compare your views on these questions:

– Can you think of at least one positive feature in you as an adult that you
  think comes from your upbringing?
– How important is early childhood for the person later on?

2 The single most important aspect in bringing up a child . . .

*'Bit **old** for a dummy isn't he?'*

Look at these statements about bringing up a child. Which ones do you agree with? Put each statement into one of these categories: a) top priority, b) quite important, c) not very important. Add other statements if you wish.

1 Children must be taught to respect authority.
2 It is important to be very firm with children.
3 It is important to show affection and love.
4 Parents should pass on family and cultural traditions to children, and teach them to respect and obey them.
5 What matters is what parents do, not what they say. They should set a good example!
6 Children should be allowed to make decisions about their lives. If they make mistakes, they can learn from them.
7 Children should always be told why they are being asked to do anything.
8 It is important to teach children to value education.
9 ....
10 ....

Find out which statements were put most often into the top priority category by the majority of students in your class. Which statements were most controversial?

3 Children and adults in a nutshell

Many people have tried to encapsulate their idea of childhood and
adulthood in very short, witty sayings. The following are ten such aphorisms
by famous people. With a partner, match the first part of each, in Column A,
with its continuation in Column B.

Column A	*Column B*
1 What is an adult?	old enough to know better.
2 Every child is	something you do if you're lucky.
3 Adults are	to be grown out of.
4 Schoolmasters and parents exist	to be alone.
5 Youth is	born a genius.
6 No man is ever	a disease from which we all recover.
7 To be adult is	A child blown up by age.
8 Growing old is	a quest.
9 Being young is	a very high price to pay for maturity.
10 Age is	obsolete children.

Compare your answers with other students. Which of the sayings do you like
best? Why?

With a partner, write an aphorism on one of these, or a topic of your choice:

- children   – parents
- students of English   – teachers of English
- ....

Pin up your aphorisms and discuss them.

>>>→

4 Conflict between children and adults

(Optional extension)

Read this short poem written from a young person's point of view.

Conflict

They say:
make up your mind;
decide;
exercise your will power;
don't go by just your feelings;
be rational.

And when I do that
they say:
don't be so stubborn;
you're so rigid;
give a little;
don't you have feelings?

Yes I do.

(Ulrich Schaffer, *For the Love of Children*)

What do you think of the poem? Do you recognise the child's views from your own childhood or adolescence?

With a partner, discuss what you would say to a child who had spoken the words of the poem. Is there any way of lessening the conflict between the generations? Compare your ideas with other students.

19 | Fostering Sally

Caring for children in difficult situations

1 Case file: Sally Emsworth

Work in small groups. Imagine that you are a team of social workers who look after children at risk in the community. Read this case file on Sally, age 5. Sally is going to be placed with a foster family.

CASE FILE

Name: *Sally Emsworth*   Age: *5*   Date of birth:

Parents: <u>Mother</u>: *Hensia Emsworth, age 24. Long history of drug abuse. In and out of drug therapy unit at Centre Hospital for the past six years. Suspected of prostitution to obtain drugs. Twice had brushes with police, but no charges resulted. Referred both times to Social Services. Diagnosed HIV positive two years ago, and needing increasing hospitalisation. Is fond of Sally but frequently leaves her on her own or is inattentive.*
<u>Father</u>: *Leon Jones, age unknown. Not been seen for nearly a year. According to Hensia, alcoholic, drug addict, unpredictable, violent, had a terrible temper. Sally was terrified of him.*

Taken into care: 9.9. Northwood Home for children. Since arrival, has been alternately silent and in a rage. Throws objects at people in charge of her - matron, visiting S. worker. Lies face down on her bed for hours. Rarely cries but often hits strangers for no apparent reason. Two attempts to run away.

Assessment: Not shy but insensitive to others. Needs to compete for attention. Has had very little contact with other children. Lived exclusively with adults. Has not experienced a stable home but lived in a range of short term accommodation. This is her first time in an institution. Has never attended school. Still wets her bed at night from time to time.

>>>→

In your 'social worker' groups, discuss the likely problems that a foster family might have with Sally. Decide what kind of foster family would be best:

— a family with one other child
— a family with other children
— a family with no other children
— young parents in their twenties
— experienced parents in their thirties or early forties
— a single parent family, with one other child

Compare and discuss your decision with other groups in the class.

2 First report on Sally's progress

The Elliott family is eventually chosen to be Sally's foster family. They live in a pleasant suburb and have two children of their own, Tommy, aged 12, and Linda, aged 17. The Elliotts have fostered children before and have always co-operated well with social worker teams. Mrs Elliott regularly phones the social workers to report on progress and to discuss any problems that arise as Sally adjusts to life in their home.

Listen to the first phone conversation about Sally. The Elliotts have been looking after her for a month.

Fill in the case notes to keep a record of the conversation. Then hold a meeting with your colleagues in your social worker team to decide on the advice and support you can give the Elliotts.

Compare and discuss your approach with another team.

3 Second phone call

 Listen to the second phone call about Sally, a month later. Take notes and discuss the situation briefly with your colleagues.

The situation does not seem to be improving. The Elliotts may not be able to continue to foster Sally. As social workers, you are now faced with a crucial decision:

— Should Sally be returned to her mother and live in some form of sheltered accommodation?
— Should the team try to find another foster family? If so, what sort of family should it be this time?
— Should Sally return to the Children's Home?

4 Meet the press

Before any decision can be carried out, Sally's mother contacts a local newspaper and declares that her rights as a mother have been taken away because she is ill. She claims that her daughter has been 'kidnapped' by the social work department. The department decides to meet the press and try to explain their actions.

Prepare for the press. With your team, decide what you are going to say about the case.

>>>→

⊟ Listen to the reporters' questions and take it in turns to give a suitable reply. Your answers will be printed in the newspapers, so it is especially important to avoid saying anything careless, too vague, or misleading.

5 Feedback and discussion

As a class, compare your feelings about the activities you have just taken part in. What do you really think the solution is for children who are at risk because of the difficult situation in which they or their parents are? Is fostering a good practice? What other possibilities are open to a community?

20 Keeping in touch

Communicating and failing to communicate

1 Communicating with far-away friends

How do people in your class communicate with far-away friends or relatives? Find out by asking three people these questions:

1 Do you have family or friends who live in distant parts?   ....
2 Would you like to be in touch more often?   ....
3 On average, how many times a month do you: ....
   – phone them?
   – write letters to them?   ....
   – send recorded cassettes to them?   ....
   – send them fax messages?   ....
   – send them postcards?   ....
   – have flowers or other gifts delivered to them?   ....

Compare your answers with other students in the class. What is the preferred way of communicating with far-away friends?

With a partner, make a list of the advantages and disadvantages of different means of communication.

	advantages	disadvantages
phone		
letters		
fax		

Compare your ideas and compile a list for the whole class.

What about the proliferation of modern means of communication? What is your reaction to these ideas?

	Great!	Ghastly!
– phones with television screens in every household	....	....
– fax machines in every hotel bedroom	....	....
– radio phones carried by everyone all the time	....	....
– telephones in all cars	....	....

Compare your views with other students and try to give reasons for them.

2 I love the phone!

You are going to listen to Bill and Judy talking about the way they communicate with friends and family. What methods of communication do they use? What do they say about them?

The speakers compare phoning and writing letters. Listen again for the advantages of writing letters.

Check your answers with another student. Did either of the speakers express ideas that are close to your own? Do you think that with the increasing use of new communication technologies, we are in danger of losing the art of letter writing? Think of reasons why we should or should not be afraid of this loss.

3 Different ways of communicating?

Different kinds of language are often needed for different means of communication. With a partner, discuss the right way of conveying the following messages if you are using other means of communication.

1 Phone: Hi! I just called to ask you to come to my party on Saturday night. Can you make it?
Letter: ....

2 Letter: I refer to your letter and would confirm that an appointment has been made for you, for 10:30 a.m. on 12th January at this office. I would be grateful if you could kindly telephone me at this office if this is not convenient.
Phone: ....

3 Fax: Confirm arrival of Managing Director on LH 0076, Hamburg 20:25. Please meet at airport and drive to Hotel Europa.
Phone: ....

Check your answers with other students.

4 On the same wavelength? Failures in communication

Does anyone in your class have a story to tell about a failure in communication, i.e. an experience when what you wanted to say just didn't get across? Or when you totally misunderstood someone else? Tell the class.

Listeners: Discuss the reasons for these failures in communication. Add other failures if you wish.

— the person trying to communicate didn't speak clearly enough
— the person communicating didn't understand the social situation
— the listener wasn't paying attention
— the listener really wanted to misunderstand
— ....
— ....

With a partner, consider these questions:

— What do you mean by 'good communication'?
— Do you think there are subjects that all people find difficult to talk about?
— Are there subjects that are difficult in your culture?
— Do you know about any other cultures where different subjects are taboo?
— Are there some subjects which are likely to cause misunderstandings between people even if they are close to each other?

Keep in touch!

We have now come to the end of our series of books on speaking skills for fluency. In small groups, share your thoughts about the experience of using the book(s), and of trying to improve your own fluency. Consider these questions:

— What has been most valuable for you?
— What did you find less useful?
— Do you think that you have improved your speaking skills – you personally, and the class as a whole?
— What do you feel you need more work on? What are your own personal difficulties in speaking?
— How can you continue to work on your spoken fluency? What are your strategies for continuing to improve and enrich your active vocabulary? How can you improve your ease of speaking? Do you feel you need daily practice? How can you achieve that?

Remember that the authors are always very pleased to hear comments, both positive and negative, from people who have used their books.
Write to:

Joanne Collie and Stephen Slater, c/o Cambridge University Press,
The Edinburgh Building, Shaftesbury Road, Cambridge CB2 2RU, UK.

Good luck with your English!

Key

Unit 3 **3.3** Suggested causes of stress: risk-taking is stressful; reduced to lower level than in native language; risk ridicule; possibility of making mistakes; possibility of being corrected; memory problems; time taken to feel any progress; regression to a lower stage of communication.

Unit 5 **5.2** 1) the director of a small language teaching company 2) an adult at university 3) a stage manager 4) a solicitor

Unit 9 **9.1** (left) The young woman is wearing aggrey and coral beads and is holding an ancuwaba doll. The beads and doll are used in a puberty rite in Ghana. (top right) The man is a geomancer (diviner) and he is divining using groundnuts in Dogon, Mali. (bottom right) This is a photo of the hands of the Bridge master's wife. Such rings are used as good luck charms in Peru. **9.4** 1 From *The Dawn of Time, Australian Aboriginal Myths in Paintings* by Ainslie Roberts with text by Charles P. Mountford, Rigby Publishers, Adelaide, 1969. The story continues: Now the kangaroo-man possessed the thigh bone of a mythical ancestor. With this bone, he had already performed many wonderful deeds. So he pointed the bone at the isthmus – the land which blocked the sea from entering the valley. The isthmus slowly split open. The sea poured through the opening, flooding the entire valley, so that the birds and the animals were forced to live together in peace.
2 Adapted from *Children of Wax, African Folk Tales*, Canongate 1989. The story continues: He returned home, took the herb, and after a week, the tree fell off his head. His wife chopped it up, used the wood for their cooking fire, and urged her husband to give the woman two cows. "I shall not," said the man. "She is just an old witch with a sharp tongue. There is no reason to give her anything."

The charm woman heard that the tree had fallen off his head and sent a young boy to tell him to send her two cows. All the man did was beat the boy with a stick and send him back home. The next day, when the man was sitting in front of his fire drinking his beer, his wife said, looking at his head, "Another tree seems to be growing, and this time it's very big." The man's heart filled with despair. He went back to the charm woman, begging her for some more magic herbs and bringing two cows for her. The charm woman shook her head. "You are a wicked man who does not keep his promises," she said. "If you want me to cure you again and stop that tree forever, you will have to pay me four cows."

The man stamped his feet in anger but he knew there was no other way of stopping the tree. Reluctantly he brought four cows. The woman gave him the herb and told him he should always keep his promises. The man said nothing, but he knew that what she said was right.

Unit 16 **16.4**
1 Mrs Roote describing her sensations when she had a heart attack and an NDE (a near death experience) in 'The Next Room' from *Sugar and Other Stories* by A.S. Byatt, Chatto & Windus 1987, Penguin Books 1988.
2 A sensitive young boy's reaction to having to work with disabled children, in 'Training' from *Dancing Girls and Other Stories* by Margaret Atwood, McClelland and Stewart 1977.
3 Mrs Dempster has just been hit by a snowball with a stone in it, thrown at the

narrator in Robertson Davies' *Fifth Business*, Penguin Books 1970.

4 Maria Takis starting to have a baby as she is held captive in Peter Carey's *The Tax Inspector*, Faber and Faber 1991.

5 The narrator wakes up the morning after the woman he loves has told him she loves someone else, in Iris Murdoch's *The Black Prince*, Chatto and Windus 1973, Penguin Books 1975.

6 A man is being interviewed by his employers to be told he is dismissed from his job. He imagines that his physical sensations are due to the employers using a Microwave Gun on him, in Iain Banks' *Walking on Glass*, Abacus 1985.

Unit 18 **18.2** The child in the cartoon has a dummy in his mouth (American English = 'pacifier'). **18.3** 1 What is an adult? A child blown up by age – *Simone de Beauvoir, French writer*. 2 Every child is born a genius – *R. Buckminster Fuller, American essayist*. 3 Adults are obsolete children – *Dr Seuss, American children's writer*. 4 Schoolmasters and parents exist to be grown out of – *Sir John Wolfenden, British politician*. 5 Youth is a disease from which we all recover – *Dorothy Fuldhelm, American writer*. 6 No man is ever old enough to know better – *Holbrook Jackson, British writer*. 7 Growing old is something you do if you're lucky – *Groucho Marx, American comedian*. 8 Being young is a quest – *V.S. Pritchett, British critic*. 9 To be adult is to be alone – *Jean Rostand, French scientist*. 10 Age is a very high price to pay for maturity – *Tom Stoppard, British playwright*.

Unit 20 **20.3**

1 I am having a party on Saturday, 27 April, from 8 p.m. onwards, at my house, 3 Belview Drive, Arden Hills, and I'd be very happy if you could come. *Or*, Mr and Mrs Blair Adro request the pleasure of your company at an evening reception to be held at 3 Belview Drive, Arden Hills, on Saturday 27 April, 18:00 to 22:00. *R.S.V.P.* (more formal)

2 Hello, I'm just calling to say that I've received your letter. We've made an appointment for you on Monday, that's the 12th of January, for 10:30 a.m. here at the office. Is that all right?

3 I'm calling to confirm that our Managing Director will arrive in Hamburg on flight Lufthansa LH 0076, at 8:25 p.m. this evening. He would be grateful if he could be met at the airport and driven to his hotel, the Hotel Europa. Thank you very much.

Tapescript

Unit 1   Secrets

2   Is gossip harmless?

1 Well, I have a terrible confession to make, in that people are always saying to me that you're such a gossip! And I say well I'm not, I'm not. It's just that when I meet people, I like to find out about them and because I'm often travelling about and meeting new people, um I sit and talk to them and I, and I ask them questions and they tell me all sorts of things about themselves and then you, then you find you say to someone, Look, don't be hard on such and such because he's really worried at the moment, because his kid's just changed school and he's really worried about it. And they say I've worked with this person for weeks and I didn't know. How did you know? And I say well, I was just talking to him and that's what he told me. So I have to say that although I don't like gossiping in general, I think it's very friendly to find out about people and know what they're up to so that you can tell other people about them.

2 I think it's very nice to listen to gossip, I have to admit. I've always got my ear open for a bit of good gossip. As long as it's not harmful to anybody. And I think it is a good point that you often learn things that are quite important to know, that you may not learn through normal conversation through someone who knows them a little better telling you a piece of information which changes the way you look at people. And you have more information about them. So as long as it's not harmful and as long as people aren't trying to hurt each other through gossip, I think it's, I think it's er quite fun. And I think people're always, if they're honest, always keeping their ears open for a nice piece of gossip about somebody they know.

3   Should you tell . . . ?

A: What if a friend er, were seeing someone else behind their partner's back or something like that and you found out about it . . .

B: Oh, I would never say anything . . .

A: Would that be something serious?

B: Oh that would be serious, yes, because it's also not, not any of my business, I don't feel. (Mm) And, I . . . and that would be, that could be very damaging . . . to them.

C: It, it depends who you're sort of closest to as well, because I mean I've been in that situation just recently and (Yeah) the, the woman was my close, close friend and then her partner was my less close friend and so er . . .

A: And it was he that was seeing someone else?

C: No, it was her that was seeing someone else, so . . .

A: Oh, it was her . . .

C: So obviously, I mean er, I kept that secret from, from him. But if it had been the other way around, and I'd found out that he was seeing somebody, then I would have told her.

B: But er, I wonder about sort of serious things, like if somebody has a serious illness, do you feel that . . . and you have been told that this this friend or relative has a serious illness, do you think that you should tell them?

A: What good would it do? In telling them that they are seriously ill if . . .

B: Well, maybe it would give them, give them time to prepare, to use what time they've got left (Mm) to the best, to . . . I wonder too, if it would stop them . . .

A: Sort of starts a chain reaction, I would imagine . . .

B: I don't know. I have a, a friend who is a little older than me who, who has cancer and she knows she has cancer and um, and is dying of it and her family all know. And um, in fact she said that this has been really good, that they, they can really sort of make the most of the time that she has left (Mm). Now I'm not certain if that's always the right thing to do, because some people might not be strong enough (Mm, I'm sure) to cope with it. But then on the other hand the strain on the family, if they had that knowledge without telling her would have been enormous, I would have thought.

C: I would have thought most people would want to know, I mean if you find out that you're ill in any way that, that's serious (Mm). The question surely at the back of your mind is how serious is it or could it be. Um . . . there's I was talking to somebody who is a doctor the other day and they said that their policy was to always, always (Mm) tell people. (Mm) Um, but er, he accepted that his . . . a lot of his colleagues would take each case as it (Yes, yes) comes, really to try and judge (Yes).

Unit 3   Stress

2   Yoga helps me to relax

A: I personally, um, do yoga when I'm really, really stressed. A large vodka tonic does help. (laughter) Sure but yoga, um, helps me to just relax enough so that I can sleep properly during the night and that . . . then I get out of that cycle of not sleeping, and not um, you know, not eating properly and, and that seems to help a little bit with me.

B: Well not sleeping is the first thing that happens to me if I'm under stress. And it's only quite recently that I've realized that, that the best thing to do is not to try to sleep. Um, what I tend to do now is I get up and make a cup of tea, camomile tea rather than tea with caffeine or tannin in it. Um, and I put on a video of something that's fairly lightweight and I will sit . . . But it's the same with all stress, really, you have to, as you say accept that you are stressed and

try and breathe deeply and be sensible. There's no point in worrying because it's not going to change anything and you have to try and think that way. It's easy to say that, it's easy to give advice, it's more difficult to actually do it. But I think I'm getting better at it.

A: One of the things that when you are stressful is you start breathing very shallow. You're not (yes) taking oxygen down into your body (overlap) panicking, (it's from up here in the neck) you tighten up and you're taking little shallow breaths, so there is (yes) you know, a, a good reasoning for that.

B: Heavy breathing . . . and deeper breaths. I think that's my sort of solution to the . . . to my stress.

Unit 4   Well brought up?

3   Talking rubbish or gibberish, or just dim-witted?

Incident 1

Well my mother told me this incident about, er, when she went into this picture framing shop. And she wanted some Indian cloth print to be framed. So she sort of walked in and er, this lady said: 'Yes madam, can I help you?' And my mum said: 'I'd like this framed. Can you suggest a frame?' And she was saying: 'Sorry? What, suggest a frame?' And obviously she couldn't understand my mother's accent and, and she was sort of talking to her as though she was deaf or speaking a completely different language. And I think it's with a lot of accents . . . and especially the English where if you do not, er, speak in an English accent they think you're either talking rubbish, gibberish, or you're dim-witted. And she was just downright rude and, and she was saying things like: 'No, I, I . . . No, you can't frame this. You've got to iron it out first. You can't bring it in like this.' And it's all sort of very patronising, and very sort of beneath and you know, sort of on a low level of talking.

Incident 2

I think the only times that I've experienced rudeness in England have been about accents. I was working once up in Edinburgh and I had rented a room in somebody's house that was kind of in the suburbs, you know, down a really tiny small street and every night when I finished work I took a taxi home because I couldn't figure out the bus system at all. So finally one night everyone talked me into taking a bus back so I got on the bus and – they said that was the right bus for where I was going. So I'm on the bus and he, he comes to a halt. And he's talking to me, in a very thick Scottish accent and I, I don't understand a word he's saying. So I was trying to be as polite as possible and saying, you know, I'm sorry, I don't understand, could you talk slower and all he did was talk louder (laughter). And, and got really you know kind of ruder each time and I, I kept saying I'm really sorry I don't understand a word, you know, you're saying. I . . . could you just explain to me how I get back, you know, and I gave him the address of where I was staying. Well evidently he was giving me directions and I didn't know that and that's what he was getting so irritated with me cause I couldn't understand the accent. And he was getting very, very crabby. And finally, he, um, you know the light that's over the bus that does the destination . . . he said an expletive and hit out the light and he drove me home in the bus. (laughter) I mean people the next day were all talking about that because it's down this little lane (laughter) and he opened the bus door and he had to like reverse and go forward about five or six times to be able to turn round and go back.

Unit 5   All in a day's work

4   My day

1   Dear Diary. Well today's the day. I have to get on the train in a few hours' time to . . . Bristol, and go and meet Sir Peter Hall at the theatre to audition for a lead on Broadway. I know now I think ahead that if I get this part it'll mean going to America to meet the head of the Schubert Organisation for them to O.K. it. But it looks promising. I've packed all my things last night, I've got to go from the theatre down to London and stay in London to perform at the National where I'm working. But this day is terribly important to me so I hope I'm ready. Er, I've looked through the play, indeed I'll look through it again on the train. But now I've got to brush my teeth and get a move on. I've got my contact lenses together, so I don't have to wear my glasses, so I look a little different. I've um put all the things in my bag and I'm going off to get the train shortly. I

must remember to take some food for the train cause I don't want to waste money on that awful British rail food . . . So off I go.

2   July the 5th, 1990. Today has been extraordinary. It's Sever's first time back in the Soviet Union and together we flew in to Moscow Airport. There were eight hundred people to meet us. There are signs . . . there were signs everywhere, there were people screaming, there were people shouting for him, there was, were photographers, the television cameras were there. We had to be smuggled out through the service entrance . . . We were pushed out through the service entrance and out to the front of the airport where all of his fans were waiting to meet him. And we stood outside the front of the airport with them for a couple of hours and then were driven into Moscow. From there we landed ourselves at the hotel, sorted out our stuff, and went out to meet his official fan club where they were camping in the woods outside Moscow, having come from all over the Soviet Union. There were over four hundred of them. We climbed into a car, and we were driven out of Moscow to these woods. And we could hear lots of people singing and having fun and we made our way towards them and it was dusk by this time. We were very tired. And they suddenly realized that Sever and I were coming to see them. And they started to go crazy and they all wanted to touch him and all wanted to talk to him. Eventually we managed to get some control and we . . . managed to get everybody sat down and for another two hours with huge bonfires burning in the middle of these woods and with them all camped around, they asked him questions, questions about everything, about his life, questions about me . . . It was absolutely extraordinary. We were exhausted but were then driven back into Moscow, and to a co-operative restaurant. At this restaurant all of the rock musicians from Moscow had come to have a special dinner with us and say hello and welcome, welcome Sever home. We sat, ate with them, talked with them, it was about 3 a.m. It's now five o'clock, and I'm at last going to be able to go to sleep. Tomorrow morning everything begins at seven so I've got two hours to rest.

Unit 6   Getting away from it all

3   They talked about it . . .

1 I think it would be quite exciting to join a community of travellers. I think it would be important that you manage to look after yourselves as much as you could and not depend on other people for charity too much, but if you could organise that somehow, particularly as a person who is fairly new to this country, I think that joining a group of travellers, being able to see all sorts of different places, each evening finding your own place to camp, and set up . . . um . . . I think often the pressures of a large community are too much for people to bear and I think sometimes it's nicer to scale down, and live in a smaller community. On a beach as well, the same sort of thing. I love the sea and I think it would be nice, too, and it's good for your mind to live by the sea.

2 I think what I've always fancied most is the, the notion of going to somewhere very remote . . . um, the Highlands of Scotland or the wilds of the West of Ireland and start a small smallholding. Er, and grow all your own vegetables, have a cow to provide milk, chickens, eggs, all that sort of thing . . . But actually, I think I'm probably being terribly romantic about it, cause I suspect it's the sort of thing that once you start it's incredibly hard work. I mean, certainly the people I know who tried to, um, be even self-sufficient in a very small way find that they're getting up at six o'clock in the morning and not getting everything done till about midnight.

Unit 7   Remember, remember

2   I'm so embarrassed when I forget someone's name

A: Nick, um . . . oh, I forgot what I was going to ask. (laughter). Do you have a good memory?

B: Um, in for some sort of areas yes I do, I think. Um and people, my friends would back me up on this, I have a sort of um good memory for dates (yeah) and um sort of slightly pedantic details about . . . oh yes, we saw that film on Tuesday the third of February and you were there and um

C: Really!

B: Yeah.

A: What about names, though, and things like that?

B: Um, that's, that's generally good as well. But um, I don't know, there's this thing about you get worse as you get older (Mm) and, and I've almost not acknowledged it but (laughter) I am aware that I'm thirty-three now . . .

A: Ooooh!

B: But . . .

A: So am I, by the way. that's not that old, is it?

B: No (laughter). No, but

A: You look older though. (laughter) Just kidding.

B: Ah no, I've just become aware that, you know, names do go. And, and whereas, and you'd be aware that you know a few, few years ago you would remember names and . . .

C: It's very strange, this thing about forgetting names. Because there are people who do seem to be totally unable to remember names (Yeah). It seems . . . I . . . I always thought that I was actually quite good at remembering names. As I get older it is getting a little bit worse. But on the whole I am quite good. But you do meet people who, who'll forget the name of somebody that they have just been talking to. (Mm, yeah). You know, and, and a name that is very familiar to them. They just don't seem to be able to hold it in their head. I don't quite understand that.

A: I have difficulty remembering names. Er, I remember faces and as you said dates and phone numbers and things like that. . . . But names. I never rem . . . And I'm never, when someone refers to me by another name, you know, I'll just correct and what not but I'm ever so embarrassed when I forget someone else's name. And I find it so difficult. But

C: It's very insulting, isn't it?

A: Yeah, it feels that way. It feels that I'm . . . (Mm) . . . exactly. It feels like I'm insulting them by not (Yes) remembering their name. (Yes) So I find when I'm introduced to someone I'll just keep going through my head, you know, repeating the name over and over and over again.

Unit 8 My brilliant career?

3 Careers advice
Conversation one

N: Judy, have you tried to give career advice in your time?

Ju: Oh yes, yes indeed, very much so at the moment. I have a daughter who is er, seventeen and a half. And she's er started on her A-levels and it's been enormously difficult to advise her, um, in what she wants to do. I think as a parent, um, your child is not going to listen to you, (No) anyway. I mean she actually wants to go into into the theatre. So anything that her father or I say is dismissed because although we work in the theatre, we . . .

B: Both of you? Your husband as well?

Ju: Yes. Well, in fact, now he actually isn't an actor any more. He was until a few years ago but now he's a Careers officer. (laughter) And he spends his day advising young people . . .

B: Not to go into the theatre!

Ju: . . . not to go into the theatre. But also on what courses they should do, and what would be suitable, and what examinations you need to have to get on to a certain course. But of course as far as his own daughter goes, um, anything that he has to say is, is completely dismissed, you know. But we have um, and she has been to our local Careers Department to talk to them and er that is a very very good service indeed and they have all the books about university courses, polytechnic courses, any kind of course. If there's er anything you want to know, there is someone there who you can go and talk to. It really is absolutely wonderful. And we found it a great help because I don't know about you, but when I was seventeen, um, girls anyway were going to be teachers or nurses um, or learn to cook and that was it. No careers advice at all.

Conversation two

Ju: Did you have careers advice, Nick, at school?

N: Um, no. And the thing I remember most um was that you had to sort of start making vague decisions in the fourth year, which is . . . I can't remember now . . . fourteen, thirteen, fourteen . . .

Ju: That's right. Yes, when you're going . . .

B: Was it that early?

N: When you select which O Levels (O Levels) which are now GCSEs, you'd have to more or less decide the direction you were going to go, sort of Arts or Sciences (Mm) and the two were not compatiblc, not in the school that I was in . . .

Ju: How does it work in the States?

Ja: In the school, in High School in America you have like a job counsellor in school that tries to . . . give you some advice and find out you know what you're good at and set you off kind of on the right path. And I can remember being told that, cause most of the kids from my High School were going on to college that it wasn't important to take er classes like, practical classes like um learning how to type, take shorthand, learning how to actually do a job which you actually can do in, in High School. And my mother didn't agree with that and said you really should learn how to do a couple – have some skills under your belt. And that was one of the best advice I had because it meant that when I was through school you know getting a career going, whatever, I had good skills to fall back on, you know. I could type. I could get a secretarial job while I was trying to get something else, while I was trying to get futher training. And if I ever see that personnel counsellor (laughter) . . . I'll tell her . . . she nearly got me on the wrong foot there . . . That's interesting, you can get very bad advice, I think.

Unit 10 Threatening times

2 The biggest threat to the planet is . . . unbridled industrialisation

1 I think the er biggest fear we all have really is, is this huge problem of global warming, of er what we human beings are doing to our own atmosphere and environment. Er, there's a report just been published that er an area of the Amazon rainforest is felled every second the size of a football pitch. Apparently every second of every day, seven days a week,

there's er that many trees disappear in the Amazon rainforest. Which means that the er whole ecological balance is being upset, the, the weather's being upset. We have these strange sudden hurricane force winds in in Great Britain which we've never had before. We have er, um, a hole in the ozone layer, skin cancer, it just is, is very frightening. Very scary and we don't know what . . . where it's going to lead or how to stop it.

2 I certainly think you're right in terms of we're much more likely to have a catastrophe, an ecological catastrophe um . . . Certainly five years ago what I was concerned about was er, a nuclear catastrophe or world war III or something. But I think the events of the last year or so have made that seem less likely (Mm). Although it's still a possibility when you consider some of the countries in the world.

3 Well I agree that it is quite worrying, um about the kind of er, I mean, both the use of nuclear fuels and, and also the ozone layer and things like that but I think that, that people have to take er into consideration that the scientific community are moving very fast now to um rectify a lot of mistakes that have been made in the past. And when you think um about all the er the new proposals that are coming in, the collecting of things which are re-usable, and er the safe disposal of fridges and such, such things and the, you know certain items like um, spray cannisters and things like that which have been er taken off our shelves, I, I think that both the scientific community and local government and also national government are looking into these problems very very carefully and are moving ahead very very fast and I don't really think we have that much to worry about.

Unit 11   Love, hope and charity

2 We'd like to feel we're doing something positive

1 I'm one of the directors of . . . it's a registered charity called Rainbow Rovers. And it was set up in conjunction with another charity called the Sahara 1A Trust. And it's unusual because it's a very specific, um charity organisation aimed at a very specific group of refugees. Which is something that attracted me to it, I think, in the first place. A lot of the bigger charities um, seem to be spread so thin by the time they get funds in and they have such high administration costs you know – 60 to 70 per cent of donated monies can go for administration and that doesn't appeal to me so much. So with Rainbow Rovers, we have really stressed that everything, practically everything everyone works for, for free – um, we get donated headquarters, um the only thing that we can't get donated so far is postage stamps. But everything else – we get a fax company to donate a fax machine, you know, everything sponsored. So that any money that the public gives to us actually buys medicines and educational supplies for this group of refugees. This specific group of refugees is, is the thing that actually brought me in. It's, it's basically about 200,000 mainly women and children, that have for fifteen years been living in er just an arid moonscape section of the Sahara desert.

2 Well in my area my mother and I are making all sorts of Indian snacks um for the charity Save the Children. Because we feel that any child who comes to this earth has a right to health, education, food, essentials like that. You know, it's really sad to see children anywhere in the world, it doesn't have to be just in the Third World areas, um, to be deprived of you know of any of those essential things. Because you know it's just appalling, like the plight of kids for example in the Sudan and also in India, Bangladesh just roaming around, you know, who don't know the joys of life and you know, sort of suffering right from the beginning of their lives. Whereas you know we all learn about suffering as we get older, whereas they begin, you know, they start by suffering from birth. So I think Save the Children Fund is my charity.

Unit 12   Buildings to look at and to work in

1 Old or new?

A: One of the buildings that comes to mind that um, I . . . I mean coming to London there are so many incredibly beautiful buildings, I mean um, coming from the States, we, we don't have anything that's older than just, you know, about two hundred years. And coming here and seeing things from, er, you know, from the eighteenth century, er, the, the seventeenth century, just . . . Saint Paul's Cathedral . . . I mean it's just amazing. And the idea that one could, um, at one time one could see that from miles away and you don't any more until you're right on it, it's such a shame. Er, a building like I said before that comes to mind is when I first came over I thought was just the ugliest thing I had ever, ever seen, I could not believe anybody could ever consider giving, giving permission to have this thing built, was the Lloyds, the Lloyds building. And, er, with these vents. And, er, er, it just looks like, er, something out of a science fiction film . . .

B: That's the one that has all its, um, insides on the outside (laughter, yes) it has the lifts on the outside and all the, the, um pipes and everything . . .

A: Yeah, it should be covered up

B: . . . on the outside.

A: But now, now I do . . . I've grown accustomed to it and there . . . I do see the appeal . . . I, I . . . there is er, I can't actually say beauty, but there is something, there is something somewhat attractive about it. (mm) And at night they, they bathe it in this violet light which, um (laughs) like I say it looks like something out of a science fiction film. But I, I do look forward to driving by it now and kind of giving it a look on the, on the way by . . . um

C: It looks very good at night as well, because they light it with a blue light, and er (yeah) that looks quite striking.

A: That's it. It is very, very striking. (yeah) And completely incongruous with everything else around it, but er . . .

3 Different people, different views . . .

A: Saw rather an extraordinary building when I was in Berlin last year. It seemed to be just the most horrible mistake. Um, it's a church . . . n . . . all I can remember is it's not far from the zoo, the entrance to the zoo. Um, I assume it had been bombed during the war. And instead of just leaving the ruins, I suppose they felt – this is West Berlin, by the way – they felt that they wanted to repair it in some way. And they have built on to it the most hideous tower full of metal and concrete and just a horrible, horrible shape. And I seem to remember there's a rather dull cross just stuck on the very top, I think I might have that wrong but . . . the whole thing is a kind of gun metal, dingy, ugly, nasty sore on what was I think once a very pretty church, judging by the very few remains.

B: I'm rather opposite to that. The one building I can think of that I, I love is the Van Gogh museum in Amsterdam. Er, and, the real . . . it's not really its architecture in terms of its shape as a building, it, it it's another reinforced concrete kind of building that you get all over the Western world and have done for the last twenty or thirty years I suppose. But it's the way that it uses the natural light, to to show off Van Gogh's paintings. And it's just, I, I, there's not a lot I can say about it, that but it, you have to really go there, but it's just stunning, because it, it's what . . . being an art gallery that was just designed for one artist's paintings also seems to be very . . . really, I mean the architect seem to have studied the paintings and thought where they should go in relation . . . (to other parts of the exhibition)

C: They, they, they actually lay out his paintings in that museum according to . . .

B: . . . chronologically. Chronologically. That's right.

C: In chronological order, so you can actually watch and see where his mind was going . . .

B: That's right . . .

C: As you're walking around. On a late summer's night (yeah) in the Van Gogh museum (yeah) when the, when the, you know the last day's light, when it's still light enough you can see everything (Mm). You kind of feel like you can see the paintings (that's right) in the same light that he might have been painting them. (yes). It is a very unusual building, that.

D: Was that, the church in Berlin you were talking about, was that the Gedächtniskirche?

A: I think it was. Because isn't it supposed to be some kind of reminder of . . .

D: That's right.

A: . . . the war?

D: Yeah. A memorial for the war, yes.

A: Yes.

D: Yes. I quite liked it (cry of horror). Mind you (laughter) . . . I like the church as a symbol, cause it's on all the postcards, it's sort of a symbol of Berlin. But also, I like the light inside. In the, in the new bit, they've got lots of blue, just, no stained glass, well just straight blue stained glass, and the whole place is suffused with this blue light. And I found that very, very peaceful. And in the middle of the city, just right in the middle of the most busy street, just to, to wander in there and sit in that blue light I really quite liked.

A: Yes I, I didn't go inside and maybe I should have done, I suppose it's rather like Coventry Cathedral, you need to go . . .

D: Oh yeah, you must go inside . . .

A: . . . inside to appreciate it.

Unit 13   Buildings to live in

2   One of the loveliest rooms I've ever been in
My friend has a house which I just love going to. The house is, the house itself is nice, it's, er, a red brick Regency house. It's, it's pretty and not, not outstandingly beautiful but the sitting room there is one of the loveliest rooms I've ever been in. And it's lovely, not particularly architecturally, it has a very pretty window, it has a window set in um, with a wide sill and the window is arched and she very often has um a a vase with some lovely flowers in it. The colours in the room are pretty. They're pale green and, and white and when I'm there I always feel good. I always feel comfortable, and I feel like the sort of person that I would like to be. And I think it's a combination of the house, the room itself, the proportions of the room, probably, but um, but also the way that she has arranged it and probably the way she herself is, her, her own um personality comes into it to make it a nice place.

Unit 15   Special cases?

3   Case study: a conflict
1 *Mother*: Well, I think um an ordinary education is a right for everyone, isn't it? And you see the special school it's so far away. We, we're not too keen on her travelling to and from school by taxi. You see, we consider that, well this makes, this automatically sets her apart from all the other children who go to school with their friends. And we've always brought her up to be as much like other kids as possible. I mean she, she's got a mind of her own and she, if she wants to do something, provided that it's possible, then she's allowed to do it. And she definitely doesn't want to go away and leave all her friends. And anyway, well naturally we'd be happier to have her here, close by.

2 *A representative of the national association for the disabled*: Well, handicapped children should be able to use local facilities and be part of the local community. And what we have in this case is a local authority which has only got one school for the physically disabled pupils and it wants all handicapped children to go to that one school. Well we believe in the basic human right of choice. So this is not good enough. What's needed is for disabled people to be able to stay in their own local communities, not be taken out of them.

3 *A representative of the local authority*: Well, we obviously want the best for Jane. We are studying her special needs. We have, I think it's fair to say, a reputation as a very caring authority, for the physically handicapped. And in many ways we have tried to allow children with handicaps to attend ordinary schools. But there are limits to what one can do when the school to which she wishes to go is so unsuitable for a child with such handicaps as Jane's. We have actually adapted Garwood Special School so that it is suitable and can offer a full curriculum to students who are in wheelchairs and who have severe physical problems. And, we could adapt, theoretically, every school in the county as well. But it would just be far too expensive.

4 *A schoolfriend of Jane's*: Well, I mean, it's crazy, isn't it. Why shouldn't she be able to come to this school just like everybody else? She was always with us in primary school, I mean, there wasn't any . . . Well it was great having her. She used to come and watch us

even on the playing fields. There wasn't ever a problem. Why should she be stuck with a lot of people she doesn't even know?

5 *The Principal of the local upper school*: Well, I'm very sorry that Jane has set her heart on coming to this school because, I have to be quite blunt, I just don't see that it's a possibility at all. Quite simply, we just don't have the facilities. In the first place, we would have to build an enormous number of ramps – you can see that here, we have a a a three storey building so it doesn't take much imagination to conceive the cost. And it, it's not just ramps. It's special lavatory facilities . . . probably even cafeteria facilities as well. Now we've got six hundred youngsters here, we have to put what resources we have into their education, not spend everything we've got on one pupil only. And let's not forget that taxpayers have already paid for the special facilities that have been built into Garwood School. It's . . . I mean you should look at it, it's a marvellous new building with all the equipment and the resources. Now at Garwood, they are in a position to offer the best training for a disabled child. We can't do that. And . . . my own opinion is that it would not be in Jane's best interests for us to try.

Unit 16   In sickness . . .

1   It was the most awful pain!

1 I guess the worst pain that I've ever had was, that I can remember is, I had an abscess in my jaw, in my tooth. And I had a, it made me run a fever at the same time so it not only the fact that it makes the whole side of your head ache that terrible ache that you get, and and frequent little stabbing pains in the region of it. But because I had a fever it felt like it went on for a lot longer than it did. It felt like you were . . . it . . . you'd never . . . you'd always been hurting and you never would stop hurting. I think that was horrible, and the relief when it was finally over was just incredible. (Mm) It was like waking up from a bad dream.

2 I think the worst pain I've ever experienced was when over the course of three days, a couple of years ago, I became completely paralysed in my legs and my arms

(Terrifying). And apart from feeling very stiff, there was the most incredible pain which was a very deep blunt pain at times, and then at other times a shooting and stabbing pain. Um, and this pain would come on every twenty minutes or half an hour and so by the time one lot of pain had actually subsided, it was, it was the next lot of pain that I was coping with. And it was quite incredible. I, I wouldn't like to experience that ever again. And yet at the same time it was quite satisfying, to actually get through that pain. (Mm)

3 The worse pain I ever had actually was in my ankle when I sprained it. And it was the second time I'd actually sprained my, my right ankle. And in fact I was hopping down some stairs and landed very badly and twisted it. And I knew immediately that it was going to be swollen beyond belief. And it was a very hot instant pain and I thought I would keep on my sock and my boot to try and keep the swelling down and a friend of mine drove me to the hospital and of course they took off the sock and boot in order to X-ray it and it was swelling before my eyes and the pain by this point had changed from the sort of stabbing to an almost like a physical bruise feeling coming out (Yes, yeah). And it was burning and so painful that even the slightest amount of weight on it . . . I mean that evening I had a sheet on it and the sheet hurt.

4 This is going to sound silly but actually the worst memory I have of pain is what eventually turned out to be nothing more than indigestion. I'd had lunch and it was one afternoon I was home looking after my – he was my only son at that time, he's my oldest son, and er suddenly I got this incredible tight feeling in my chest. I immediately thought the worst, I thought it was going to be a heart attack or whatever. And it got worse and worse, and I was, I literally couldn't move. And my younger son . . . my son who was about three at the time was in the room with me. And he made it worse, because he found this extraordinarily funny. (laughter) There was Daddy, rolling about or writhing on the bed moaning in pain and he just was in hysterics the whole time.

Unit 17 . . . And in health

3 What is your experience of . . . ?

1 Well, I suffer from all sorts of weird allergies and things like that or seem to, so I've been the round of the alternative medicines a bit because, sort of conventional medicine really doesn't help a lot in those areas it seems. And, um, sometimes I've had encouraging results, sometimes less so. I've done quite a lot of acupuncture, which I quite enjoy, partly because I like the, the lady who gives it to me, I think it's nice to have your hand held for an hour but um, I must admit it does hurt a bit when the needles go in . . . And although she thinks I've made great progress, I'm not quite sure . . . if I've experienced it myself. So I don't go to that so often now. Um, I've had homeopathy at various stages and er recently I've been seeing an Ayurvedic doctor who is the traditional Indian form of medicine. And he combines homeopathy with physical exercises, with diet, etc. And he's good for a laugh . . . There's all sorts of spiritual input as well . . . Um, and on the more physical side, two things I've done which I have found useful. One is the Alexander technique, which is, er, which is about posture and well, a bit more than posture really, but, um, how you stand and how you do things and . . . inhibiting your automatic responses and bad habits. And the other is a form of very heavy massage, called Rolfing, um which is very painful at times but actually I did find very satisfying, very useful.

2 I've er, I've had some contact with alternative medicine, mainly the . . . er macrobiotics. Um I did a brown rice diet about, oh about oh twelve or fifteen years ago, something like that. I had er, I had um stomach ulcer problems and um er . . . and immediately went on the strictest regime which was ten days eating nothing but brown rice. Which I did, and um it did actually sort my stomach out incredibly quickly. Um . . . I then, I kept up with it for about a year er, cause you slowly begin to add other, other ingredients to the diet and I found it, I must say I did feel really good but I've just sort of lapsed out of it and drifted away from it. Um, I've also had acupuncture which I had er partly cause I had a skin problem as well but also to try and give up smoking. Er and that and that was terrific um . . . And I had the acupuncture, and then I read a book as well about giving up smoking and, and I stopped smoking, that was four years ago now . . . so, so that worked.

3 Acupuncture – I've had it myself – and I find it very efficient, but it's a bit aggressive sometimes. And you find yourself well before you're prepared to be well. Er, you don't actually get a chance to recover. Um, it's quite dynamic. Um, and I found that Shiatsu suited me better. So it's, it's a massage, um it gives pressure along the meridians, along the health points. But it also stretches out muscles and ligaments and eases back pain and that kind of thing . . . it's generally energy giving.

4 Well I'm from California so I like to try everything. (laughter) It's just in my nature and my soul. I've had acupuncture, which I enjoyed and I thought it helped me but . . . er, there's something that is not . . . I didn't find so relaxing about it . . . But my favourite alternative medicine that I've done so far or system has been reflexology . . . where they use there's different points. Basically, they use your foot but a lot of other different places in your body, on your body with um using different oils and pressure points on the feet that are supposed to correspond to different organs in your body or you know, skin or everything. And that I have found incredibly beneficial. I mean, at first I found it very painful but it doesn't hurt as much now and it really, it . . . the reason that I went, you know to go to the reflexologist in the first place, it's actually cleared up you know that whole problem so I've enjoyed that a lot.

Unit 19 Fostering Sally

2 First report on Sally's progress

Mrs Elliott: It's . . . er . . . it's Molly Elliott here, I'm fostering Sally . . . Sally Emsworth. I'd just like to bring you up to date with what's been going on since Sally came to live with us. And, er just ask for some response from you . . . some advice maybe. Well, er as we expected, Sally has not settled very quickly. She stays in her room a lot, says very little to any of us . . . er she looks rather accusingly at me when she asks where her mum is. She has been wetting the bed most nights. And hides when I change the sheets. I'm giving her plenty of physical contact . . . hugs, holding her hand, that sort of thing. But she doesn't react positively to that, and she usually struggles to get free. Oh, yes, she's been stealing a few things from drawers . . . nothing very valuable: bits of money, jewellery, always small things. She always gives them back when I find them but she says she didn't take them. Er, and one night I caught her eating bread and jam in the kitchen, about two o'clock in the morning. . . . She's been rather unkind to our dog. I saw her throwing stones at her yesterday. Well I told her firmly not to do it. She took no notice and she just said: 'I want my mum.' And that was quite soon after her last visit to the hospital. What do you think? I'd really appreciate a meeting soon to talk over things. Could you give me a ring? Thanks. Bye.

3 Second phone call

Mrs Elliott: Hello . . . er Mrs Molly Elliott here again. You never seem to be around when I call. No doubt you've got a heavy caseload. Well, it's about Sally again. It's really getting a bit much for us. Er . . . where shall I start . . . um school . . . Sally's been at school for three days now but er she has run away every day . . . well not far, just down to the shops to 'borrow' one or two things, sweets, and cigarettes for her mum mainly. And she still doesn't trust me, and her tantrums are getting worse. She has been throwing things at the wall in her room. The bedside lamp got broken the other day. Thank goodness it wasn't plugged in. We're really trying very hard, all of us, giving her lots of love and support. But she just won't accept us. And it's heartbreaking to see such an angry wee girl. My husband is wondering whether she should go back into institutional care. But I'm sure a stable home is what she really needs, a safe place to get sorted out and to have time to respond to love . . . oh, and one other thing, one ray of light perhaps. Sally has been crying a little bit this week, her first tears. And she actually let me hug and comfort her for a little while afterwards. My own kids are getting a bit fed up with her.

They were marvellous at the beginning but . . . Sally does get most of my time and attention and they are feeling it. I'm not sure it's fair on them. What do you think? Can we talk it over as a family with you? Er, please give me a ring. I'm not sure what Sally will be into next and I can't watch her twenty-four hours a day.

4 Meet the press

1 Doesn't a mother have a right to be with her child for as long as she wishes, especially when she is ill?
2 How is Sally at present?
3 Don't you think children have rights? Not to be separated from their mother, for example?
4 Have you got any idea what it is like to be separated from your mother when you are a young child and and don't understand why?
5 Then what do you say to the accusation that social workers are insensitive to people's feelings because they are the servants of rules and regulations?
6 But following on from that, aren't you making matters worse by interfering in Sally's life?
7 Is there any truth in the rumour that the foster family want Sally to leave?
8 And what are your immediate plans for Sally?
9 And are you, are you at all optimistic about Sally's future?
10 Why is Sally not living with her mother, given that hospitals have facilities for families?

Unit 20   Keeping in touch

2 I love the phone!

B: I love the phone. I love the immediacy of the, of er telephoning up er family and friends. Um, as I'm from the States, I'm, I'm quite a ways away and and er just gabbling on. But I also do love getting letters from from people and er, er the . . . one is able to er, for me I love getting it. I find myself er a bit re, er . . . I don't write enough so I don't get the letters in return. Er, but when I do write I find that I'm able to er express more, more er thoughts and feelings, in more detail and er it's also very much of a er um, in a way a cathartic thing. I tend to, I'm able to almost self-analyse but er hmm . . . Have you ever done a recorded cassette?

J: I tried to. Some years ago when my sister was living in Cyprus we thought that this would be a very good way to communicate. But it never really, it never really worked. I know that people do, and find it very satisfactory but it's not um, not really my thing. Like you, I, I use the phone, mostly. I have people who I communicate with once a year on Christmas cards. And then I, on the back of the Christmas card I write a sort of brief resume of what's been going on, um in the year. Um, and just recently I have been writing more letters. My parents are very elderly and not in very good health now so I phone them fairly frequently to find out how things are. But I've also decided to er write to them at least once a week, because I can tell them things in more detail than I would on the phone. They've also got a letter to sit over and read again. It will take up more time in their day, which I think is important. Um, and er also they very often forget things that I say on the phone, so maybe in a letter they might, they might remember it a bit more. And people send me postcards when they go on holiday and I love that, so I always try and send people postcards too.

To the teacher

This book has been written to encourage the development of fluency in spoken English and is intended for students who have reached an advanced level. Having built a secure foundation of grammatical forms and vocabulary, learners at this level have more resources with which to express their own thoughts and feelings. In many cases, however, they still need to develop their ability to operate on a more abstract level of argument and discourse. Many of them will now wish to participate in more extended discussion in their new language, or give presentations connected with their occupation or field of study. For this reason, several of the topics around which the present volume has been structured address issues that it is hoped will be productive of argument or debate, and that require lengthier or more organised spoken production from the learner. There is also a unit specifically designed to help learners improve their public speaking by becoming aware of their strengths and building upon them.

Despite this increased emphasis on more formal types of speaking, the main focus of the exercises remains fluency and ease of communication, as in the first three books in the series. At the advanced level, developing fluency still implies taking risks, being willing to experiment with language in a relaxed, friendly atmosphere – an atmosphere of trust and support. In the classroom, this can best be achieved if teacher and learners share a belief that says, 'What you are saying is more important to me than how accurately you are saying it.'

The format of *Speaking 4* follows that of *Speaking 3* in attempting to vary the kinds of speaking required of learners. Some units suggest group projects that take students out of the classroom, for example to complete surveys of community attitudes, or to gather information for guide booklets or cassettes. Class exhibitions, poster displays, writing poems and performing 'radio programmes' or commercials are other ways of varying class feedback and generating more discussion. These may be more suitable for some classes than for others, and are occasionally suggested as optional extensions at the end of a unit. Our own experience and that of many of the teachers who piloted this material is that this type of activity often works surprisingly well, even with unlikely classes, producing tangible benefits in the form of increased student solidarity.

As in *Speaking 3*, some of the units in this book are thematically paired (units 12/13, 16/17, and 18/19). These can be used to extend work on a theme if that is appropriate to a particular class or learning situation, or they can be used independently of each other. There are some exercises which encourage students to experiment with different methods in class (units 3 and 7) or which embody simulations in which learners are asked to imagine that they are part of an ongoing situation and to respond to it with their own thoughts and decisions (units 6, 15 and 19). In all of these, the aim is to encourage students to use language in more extended interactions with others, either in the environment of the classroom, or in imagined situations focusing on moral or social dilemmas.

The cassette

You will find the materials available on the cassette marked by ⬛.

We believe that an ability to deal with unsimplified spoken English is a vital accompaniment to the development of spoken fluency. However, in order to avoid overburdening the students' capacities for comprehension, many of our listening tasks require understanding only at the level of gist.

As in the earlier books, the listening materials are of several types. Some of the materials have accompanying gist comprehension tasks, for example, matching exercises, note-taking or retelling the main points. Most listening pieces lead learners on to making spoken comparisons with their own situation. In some of the simulations, listening extracts comprise part of the action and are thus integral. These extracts sometimes require more detailed comprehension.

Where listening tasks have specific answers, these can be found in the tapescript.

The listening materials in this book include speakers from a variety of nations and thus provide a rich base for the comprehension of spoken English.

Students working together

All our units invite students to talk with one another in small groups or in pairs. Being in a classroom learning a language is essentially a social experience and should be memorable, in part, because of the relationships forged during a time of being and learning together. In fluency work one of our aims is to make learners less conscious of their vulnerability in the target language by tempting them to become interested in the people in the classroom and therefore more willing to take risks to satisfy their curiosity.

Encouraging fluency in the classroom

Fluency materials, especially those that explore personal topics, rely on the skill of the teacher in easing students into the themes and in setting an atmosphere of trust and respect. Sensitivity to the needs and desires of a particular class becomes more important than ever when teachers come to select a theme or unit and begin to orient their students to it. It is vital that the topic should intrigue and engage students so that they are keen to share their own ideas and feelings about it with others in the group.

In piloting this material, we found that some classes responded very positively to what might be considered rather serious issues, while others were not in the mood for them. The teacher is best placed to find and choose the right material for particular students. Nevertheless, we hope that the units in this book will provide enough variety to enable teachers to find suitable material for different types of classes.

The preliminary care needed to choose appropriate themes and to create a classroom atmosphere that is relaxed and supportive is probably useful for most areas of language work – but where the aim is specifically to foster fluency, it is indispensable. Whereas learners can attain accuracy by doing a series of exercises in step with others in the class, they are unlikely to become more fluent unless they 'do their own thing' and become motivated to communicate something of their own thoughts and experiences. Talking about topics in which they take a personal interest and about which they care allows them to associate their new language with their own lives, and this is particularly important when the learners are learning English in their own country. It also strengthens and enriches the quality of social contact in the classroom and widens the boundaries of interaction involving the target language.

Choosing and adapting material

We encourage teachers to be bold in selecting activities and ideas from this book and adapting them to their teaching styles and to the type of classes and students that they have. The book provides a framework only, and experiment is sometimes the only way to find the most suitable methods or materials for particular learners.

Cultural location

Our material tries to cast a wide geographical net rather than be centred exclusively in British or other English-speaking locations. In many of the units students are asked to talk in English about their home towns, villages or cities, or about the environment in which they are now living. This seems consistent with a belief that students can talk more easily and flexibly about places they know well.

We wish you an interesting and fruitful time with the activities in this book and welcome comments and reactions from teachers who use these materials.

Acknowledgements

The authors and publishers are grateful to the following individuals and institutions for permission to reproduce copyright material. It has not been possible to identify the sources of all the material used and in such cases the publishers would welcome information from copyright holders.

p. 1 extract from *Collins COBUILD Dictionary* published by HarperCollins Publishers; pp. 8–9 'Stress – is your life a blur?' by David Nicholson-Lord, *The Independent on Sunday*; p. 30 'One for the storehouse' from *Gifts from my grandmother* by permission of Meiling Jin and Sheba Feminist Press; p. 35 extracts from leaflet PL773 by permission of the Department of Employment. This material is Crown copyright; p. 40 adaptation from 'Head Tree' from *Children of Wax, African Folk Tales* (1989) by Alexander McCall Smith, published by Canongate Press; p. 66 extract from a brochure produced by the British Heart Foundation, 14 Fitzhardinge Street, London W1H 4DH, charity number 225971; p. 67 (1) extract from 'The next room' in *Sugar and Other Stories* by A.S. Byatt, by permission of Peters Fraser & Dunlop and Chatto & Windus, (2) extract from *Dancing Girls and Other Stories* by Margaret Atwood. Used by permission of the Canadian publishers McClelland & Stewart, Toronto, also permission granted by Margaret Atwood, (3) extract from *Fifth Business* by Robertson Davies (Penguin Books, 1977) copyright © Robertson Davies 1970, reproduced by permission of Penguin Books Ltd, (4) extract from *The Tax Inspector* by Peter Carey (1991) by permission of Faber and Faber Ltd, Random House Inc. and University of Queensland Press, (5) extract from *The Black Prince* by Iris Murdoch (1973) by permission of Chatto & Windus and Peters Fraser & Dunlop, (6) extract from *Walking on Glass* by Iain Banks (1985) published by Macmillan London Ltd; p. 70 'Big hand for a small miracle' © Antony Beevor.

For permission to reproduce photographs and illustrations: p. 1 'The gossipers' by Paul Gaugin: Zefa; p. 3 copyright © BBC; p. 4 Gateshead College; p. 10 photograph by Fausto Dorelli and pp. 10–11 illustrations all reproduced from *The Book of Stress Survival* by Alix Kirsta published by Unwin Hyman (1986) and Thorsons (1992) with the kind permission of

Gaia Books Ltd; p. 12 illustration by Nigel Paige, illustration and two short extracts from *Drama Techniques in Language Learning (New Edition)* by Alan Maley and Alan Duff, published by Cambridge University Press (1982) by permission of the authors and publisher; p. 13 © Vivian Knox-Thompson/Statics; p. 15 Peter Ducker; p. 21 (top left) Zefa, (centre right) James L. Amos/Zefa, (top right) Eric Riddick/Images Colour Library, (bottom left) Images Colour Library; p. 25 jacket to *Castaway* by Lucy Irvine featuring a photograph by Gary Steer by permission of Victor Gollancz; p. 27 cartoon by Frank Gotham by kind permission of *Punch*; p. 30 'Old woman reading' by Rembrandt in the collection of the Duke of Buccleuch and Queensbury KT; p. 31 Pete Saloutos/Zefa; p. 33 Len Tomnie/Solihull Careers Service; p. 36 (left) Juliet Highet/Brimah, Hutchison, (top right) Hutchison, (bottom right) H.R. Dorig/Hutchison; p. 39 Dale Roberts, Art Australia for the drawing by Ainslie Roberts from *The Dawn of Time*; p. 40 sketch of an *oda* tree by Ibrahim N. Shariff from the cover of *The Oromo of Ethiopia: A History 1570–1860* by Mohammed Hassen, published by Cambridge University Press (1990), reproduced by permission of the publisher; p. 42 leaflet cover, copyright Friends of the Earth; p. 43 © Greenpeace Ltd/James; p. 45 (top) leaflet, copyright Greenpeace Ltd, (bottom) Save The North Sea Campaign; p. 46 ActionAid; p. 47 Cambridge Newspapers Ltd; p. 49 (top) British Tourist Authority, (bottom) Lloyd's Building photographed by Janet Gill; p. 52 (top) Rijksmuseum Vincent van Gogh, (bottom) Kaiser-Wilhelm-Gedächtniskirche and new buildings by Egon Eiermann, photographs by Brodersen/Berlin Tourist Office; p. 54 (top) Kawai Kanjiro's House, (bottom) Justin Slee/Guzelian; p. 61 (top) Charlotte Winn, (bottom) Disabled Young Adults Centre, Exeter; p. 65 Mary Evans Picture Library; p. 70 Antony Beevor; p. 73 (left) Scottish Television, (right) 'Feeding Hungry Kids', The Children's Aid Society; p. 74 cartoon from *Toddler* by Ros Asquith, published by Fontana, an imprint of HarperCollins Publishers Ltd;

Drawings by Tim Beer, pp. 62, 77, 78, 79; Chris Evans, pp. 41, 51; Harriet Dell, p. 14; Leslie Marshall, pp. 24, 28, 29, 32, 37, 64; Chris Pavely, p. 83; Chris Rothelo, pp. 23, 56 and Shaun Williams p. 84. Photography by Nigel Luckhurst pp. 19, 38, 68; Jeremy Pembrey, p. 57. Text artwork by Peter Ducker.

Book design by Peter Ducker MSTD.